SHOW AND TELL

OTHER BOOKS BY JIM DANIELS

Factory Poems
On the Line
Places/Everyone
The Long Ball
Digger's Territory
Punching Out
Hacking It
M-80
Niagara Falls
Blessing the House
No Pets (fiction)
Blue Jesus
Red Vinyl, Black Vinyl
Greatest Hits
Digger's Blues
Night with Drive-By Shooting Stars
Detroit Tales (fiction)

Books edited by Jim Daniels:

Punchin' Out with the Mill Hunk Herald
    (coedited with the Mill Hunk Herald cooperative)
Carnegie Mellon Anthology of Poetry
American Poetry: The Next Generation
    (coedited with Gerald Costanzo)
Letters to America: Contemporary American Poetry on Race

SHOW
AND TELL

New and Selected Poems

Jim Daniels

THE UNIVERSITY OF WISCONSIN PRESS

The University of Wisconsin Press
1930 Monroe Street
Madison, Wisconsin 53711

www.wisc.edu/wisconsinpress/

3 Henrietta Street
London WC2E 8LU, England

5   4   3   2   1

Text and jacket design by Mira Nenonen
Printed in the United States of America

Library of Congress Cataloging-in-Publication Data
Daniels, Jim, 1956–
Show and tell: new and selected poems / Jim Daniels.
        p.   cm.–(University of Wisconsin Press poetry series)
        ISBN 0-299-18580-X (hardcover: alk. paper)–
        ISBN 0-299-18584-2 (pbk.: alk. paper)
I. Title. II. Brittingham prize in poetry (Series).

PS3554.A5635 S56   2003
811'.54–dc21
                                    2002152711

CONTENTS

ACKNOWLEDGMENTS

Grateful acknowledgment to the original publishers of the books in which many of these poems first appeared:

"My Father Worked Late," "No Job," "Digger Drives to Work," "Digger Goes Hunting," "Digger Goes on a Vacation," "Short-Order Cook," "May's Poem," "Work Shoes," "Factory Love," and "After Work," from *Places/Everyone* by Jim Daniels, © 1985. Reprinted by permission of the University of Wisconsin Press.

"Where I'm at: Factory Education," "Midnight Date," "Work Boots: Still Life," "Soo Locks," "Work Song: Blues for Me, Blues for Jeannie," and "Work Song: Factory Musical," from *Punching Out,* by Jim Daniels, © 1990. Reprinted by permission of Wayne State University Press.

"M-80," "Crazy Eddie," "Parked Car," "Anthem," "Digger Ties One On," "Digger's Territory," "Time, Temperature," "Broke," and "Trouble at the Drive-In," from *M-80,* by Jim Daniels, © 1993. Reprinted by permission of the University of Pittsburgh Press.

"Niagara Falls," from *Niagara Falls,* by Jim Daniels, © 1994. Reprinted by permission of Adastra Press.

"Blessing the House," "Birch Bark," "My Mother See-Through Blouse," "Sin Sandwich," "Polish-American Night, Tiger Stadium," "How," "Night Light," "Coming Home from the Hospital after My Son's Birth," "Silk," and "The Sleeper Hold," from *Blessing the House,* by Jim Daniels, © 1997. Reprinted by permission of the University of Wisconsin Press.

"Yellow Jesus," "Green Jesus," "Purple Jesus," "White Jesus," "Night Janitor, McMahon Oil," "The Fall," "Shedding the Vestments," "Bone and Hook," "The Black Hole of the Human Body," "Evolution: Two Figures with Monkey," and "Jet of Water," from *Blue Jesus,* by Jim Daniels, © 2000. Reprinted by permission of Carnegie Mellon University Press.

"Red Vinyl," "Quitting the Card Club," "Heat Wave," "Helping with My

Brother's Résumé," "Beautiful Thing," "Falling Bricks," "Between Periods," and "Brown's Farm," from *Night with Drive-By Shooting Stars,* by Jim Daniels, © 2002. Reprinted by permission of New Issues Press.

"Digger on the Nature Trail" and "Digger Laps at the Bowl," from *Digger's Blues,* by Jim Daniels, © 2002. Reprinted by permission of Adastra Press.

Sincere acknowledgment also to the original publishers of the new and previously uncollected poems:

Indiana Review and *A Gathering of Poets,* Ed. Maggie Anderson, Alex Gildzen; Kent State University Press: "A Real Comedian: The True Genius of Bob Hope"
For a Living: Poetry of Work, Ed. Peter Oresick, Nicholas Coles; University of Illinois Press: "The Tenured Guy"
Michigan Quarterly Review: "Skywriting"
Gettysburg Review: "The Beginnings of Compassion"
Portland Review: "The Facts of Grief"
Virginia Quarterly Review: "The Church of Mr. Pea"
Heart: "Econo"
Triquarterly: "Flag Day in Warren, Michigan"
Red Brick Review: "Sock-Hop Blues"
Sycamore Review: "The Sound of It"
Quarterly West: "Show and Tell"

The poems are arranged in chronological order by book, with the exception of the Digger poems, which originally appeared in *Places/Everyone, Digger's Territory, M-80,* and *Digger's Blues.* Since these poems follow the character Digger as he ages, it seemed appropriate to put the selected Digger poems together in one section of this volume.

Note: "Bone and Hook," "The Black Hole of the Human Body," "Evolution: Two Figures with Monkey," and "Jet of Water" from *Blue Jesus* were written in response to the paintings of Francis Bacon. The title of each painting appears beneath the corresponding poem's title.

While there are too many individuals to thank for their help with various poems included in this volume, I would like to thank Kristin Kovacic and Marc J. Sheehan for their assistance in the selection process.

SHOW AND TELL

1

PLACES/EVERYONE

MY FATHER WORKED LATE

Some nights we were still awake
my brother and I, our faces smearing the window
watching the headlights bounce up the driveway
like wild pitches of light
thrown by a tired moon.
We breathed in the huge silence
after the engine died
then ran to the door, grabbing his legs
as if we could hold him there
through night, morning, forever.

Some nights when he wasn't too tired
he took off his shirt
and sat in the middle of the floor.
We wrestled, trying to pin
back his arms, sitting on his chest,
digging our heads into the yellow stains
under the arms of his t-shirt.
Each time we thought we had him—
do you give, huh, do you give?—
he sat up, cradling us both in headlocks
in the closest thing to an embrace
that I remember, and carried us to bed.

Other nights he looked right through us
mechanically eating his late dinner
yelling at anything that moved.
Some mornings we woke to find him
asleep on the couch, his foreman's tie
twisted into words we couldn't spell.
We ate our cereal as carefully as communion
until our mother shook him ready for another day.

■

My father carries no wallet full of lost years
carries no stubs, no guarantees, no promises.

We could drive toward each other all night
and never cross the distance of those missing years.

Today, home for a visit,
I pull in front of the house.
My father walks down the steps
limping from his stroke
he is coming toward me
both of us pinned to the wind
he is looking at me as if to say
give, give, I give,
as if either of us
had anything left to give.

NO JOB

Laying off, they're laying off
softball teams swinging
their bats suddenly heavy
the ball so small.

A ton of robots in his dream
march across the field
men nervously put
out their cigars.

Tire tracks across his lawn
faded stripes, dead tiger
old soldier not sure
about the war, any war.

He drinks Mad Dog
he smokes homegrown
he sits naked with the want ads
he barks up the wrong tree.

He wants to skin himself
hang his hide out to dry
bugs, sticky dimes crawling on his arms
there's no jobs, no no no jobs.

He burns a cigarette
into the arm of his chair
his oldest child
his father, the sofa.

A woman shrinks his house
with a vacuum cleaner.
It's his wife
she sucks him up.

He sells his car, buys a junker
he sells his records, has a garage sale

he gets rid of his dog: tiny hairs
he'll never be gone.

He circles the block, sun
drying him out. Neighbors
his age, younger, older: raisins.
They nod, no jobs.

High school, toking up behind auto shop
parking lot sticky tar in the heat.
Ford, Chevy, Chrysler—
where you gonna work?

Sweat darkens his shirt. Back home
he drains a beer, sucking something
down at last. His father got him in: greasy
coveralls. Nice check. Car. Wife. House.

She cooks mac and cheese
she cooks dented cans
he goes for long walks
he never gets lost.

He yanks out
all the bushes in his yard
swinging a shovel at the roots.
He chases the paperboy.

Television smashed in the driveway.
His wife hides with neighbors.
No, no, no jobs:
he throws his knife in the air.

SHORT-ORDER COOK

An average joe comes in
and orders thirty cheeseburgers and thirty fries.

I wait for him to pay before I start cooking.
He pays.
He ain't no average joe.

The grill is just big enough for ten rows of three.
I slap the burgers down
throw two buckets of fries in the deep frier
and they pop pop, spit spit . . .
pssss . . .
The counter girls laugh.
I concentrate.
It is the crucial point—
they are ready for the cheese:
my fingers shake as I tear off slices
toss them on the burgers/fries done/dump/
refill buckets/burgers ready/flip into buns/
beat that melting cheese/wrap burgers in plastic/
into paper bags/fried done/dump/fill thirty bags/
bring them to the counter/wipe sweat on sleeve
and smile at the counter girls.
I puff my chest out and bellow:
Thirty cheeseburgers! Thirty fries!
I grab a handful of ice, toss it in my mouth
do a little dance and walk back to the grill.
Pressure, responsibility, success.
Thirty cheeseburgers, thirty fries.

MAY'S POEM

"I want to write a poem
about something beautiful,"
I tell May the cook.
On my break from the grill
I stand against the open kitchen door
getting stoned.

"That shit make you stupid."
May wrinkles her forehead
in waves of disapproval.

"I don't need to be smart
to work here." The grease
sticks to my skin, a slimy
reminder of what my future holds.

"I thought you was gonna be
a writer. What about that
beautiful poem?"

I take a long hit
and pinch out the joint.
"You'll end up no good
like my boy Gerald."

"May, I'm gonna make you
a beautiful poem," I say
and turn and grab her
hug her to me, pick her up
and twirl her in circles
our sweaty uniforms
sticking together, her large
breasts heaving in my face
as she laughs and laughs
and the waitresses all come back
and the dishwasher who never smiles

makes a noise that could be
half a laugh.

But she's heavy
and I have to put her down.
The manager stands there:
"Play time's over."
Everyone walks away—
back to work.

This isn't my beautiful poem, I know.
My poem would have no manager,
no end to breaks. My poem
would have made her lighter.
My poem would have never put her down.

THE GOOD PARTS

Loaned out to another department for the day
I had a job painting the good parts green,
the bad orange.

When the line broke down
I painted my shoes green
and danced a resurrection from grease.

I was Mr. Greenshoes,
my feet so light and new
I painted my socks too.

Foreman said "Asshole,"
spit on the floor, asked me
to work late.

I said, "Greenshoes don't want
no overtime!" danced for him
followed his thumb to the door.

FACTORY LOVE

Machine, I come to you 800 times a day
like a crazy monkey lover:
in and out, in and out, in and out.

And you, you hardly ever break down,
such clean welds, such sturdy parts.
Oh how I love to oil your tips.

Machine, come home with me tonight.
I'll scrub off all the stains on your name,
grease and graffiti.

I'm tired of being your part-time lover.
Let me carry you off
into the night on a hi-lo.

That guy on midnights,
I know he drinks,
and beats you.

AFTER WORK

On this night of blue moon and damp grass
I lie bare-backed on the ground
and hum a children's song.
The air is cool for midnight, July.
The grass pins my sticky back.

You, moon, I bet you could fill
my cheeks with wet snow
make me forget I ever touched steel
make me forget even
that you
look like a headlight
moving toward me.

2 *PUNCHING OUT*

WHERE I'M AT: FACTORY EDUCATION

My first week, I'm working the cover welder
when the automatic welding gun stops
being automatic halfway through a cover.

I rush down the aisle, biting my lip, sweat
in my eyes, to find Santino the foreman.
The other guys stop working to watch.
Santino gets Old Green, the job setter
to fix my machine.

Later, Spooner grabs my neck
pushes my face into the wall.
Old Green shouts into my ear:
You ain't supposed to get Santino,
he's got to find you, dig?
What's the big hurry, boy?
You get paid the same no matter.
Kissing ass good way to get
your lips burned.
He walks away. Spooner lets go.
He stands, shaking his head:
where you at, brother, where you at?

::

Santino shows me a new job:
after the machine cuts the tubes
hang them on these hooks.

I pick them up, hang them,
pick, hang, till the edges slice
moons into my hands. I stop.
The line backs up.

Santino slaps my bloody hands,
grabs my shirt: *where's*
your goddamn gloves?

The plant nurse tapes my hands.
When I return, Santino throws me
leather gloves: *next time*
you're fired.

I shove anger deep
into rough leather. I forget
and work fast.

Where you at, brother?

■■

Bush idles over from his broken press
big pot sticking out tight
under a white t-shirt
gray hair slicked back, perfect.
He bends toward me and stares
at my greasy coveralls. I sweat
behind the washer, tossing
axle housings onto pallets.

Hey, look at me. Am I dirty?
Am I sweating?
You gotta learn how to survive
around here, kid. If you don't know
how to break your machine
then you shouldn't be running it.
He spits on the floor, wanders away.

I push safety glasses up my nose.
The parts start backing up
so I toss them sloppy into baskets,
pause to straighten the rows,
get farther behind.

A part glides crooked down the conveyor
and I rush to straighten it,
but catch myself. It catches
on the washer's inside edge.

Parts pile up behind the jammed piece.
The conveyor chain clicks, then snaps.
I press the *stop* button.

Bush passes by, smiling,
patting his belly.
Sit your ass down, kid.
When Santino comes
look stupid. Like this.

■■

Santino rushes over. His shirt says
"Your Safety Is *Our* Business."
You bet I work safely—I just point
to the machine, and thumbs down.
He can't touch it—it's not his job.
See if you can fix it, he says.
Not my job, I say.
He calls Old Green
who looks at it and says
Not my job—need an electrician.
Electrician shows up
but he just wants to jive
with Nita, the fox at the next press.
Santino gets on his case
which *is* his job
and the electrician
fixes the machine
which is *his* job
and I go back to my idiot buttons.
Which is *my* job.
I work safely.

Where you at?

MIDNIGHT DATE

After calling you on my last break
I watch the sun set over rolls of steel
rusting in the factory yard.

Old Green lies on greasy cardboard,
hands folded over his chest.
He opens his eyes, glances at me,
closes them again.

I close my eyes and see your shiny hair
fall across my face. Santino calls me
back, shoots me with a finger.

■

I put on earphones, safety glasses,
shove my hands into sweaty leather
and stand in dim light waiting
for axle housings to rattle down
the line, drop their gray weight
into my hands. I throw my head back
and howl your name: two more hours.

■

Santino gives the *break* sign.
I toss my gloves in a barrel,
punch my card, wash up.

I leave the locker room
with clean hands and step out
into what I want to believe
is a sky full of good will,
is a parking lot lined with possibility.

Tonight the moon looks full enough
to feed a lot of hearts. Mine rises
like the bird furthest from this factory.

Tonight let's shed our clothes
and dance in this cool air.
Let's taste the moon's
clean white meat.

WORK BOOTS: STILL LIFE

Next to the screen door
work boots dry in the sun.
Salt lines map the leather
and laces droop
like the arms of a new-hire
waiting to punch out.
The shoe hangs open like the sigh
of someone too tired to speak
a mouth that can almost breathe.
A tear in the leather reveals
a shiny steel toe
a glimpse of the promise of safety
the promise of steel and the years to come.

SOO LOCKS

-for my mother

You talk about the Soo Locks
and how you love to watch the water
go up and down, and the boats,
and I laugh, *The water goes up*
and down, big deal, and grab
the lunch you made me
and run out the door
and drive to the job
to stack steel
and I watch the press go up and down
and the more it goes up and down
the more steel I have to stack.
I understand this factory up and down,
simple and American, machines and steel,
and I eat the lunch you made me
and close my eyes
and try to picture the water
going up and down.

WORK SONG: BLUES FOR ME, BLUES FOR JEANNIE

A beautiful woman works
down the line from me
dressed in baggy coveralls
but still you can see.

Closest I've been, she was
slamming brakes with me.
Closest I've been—
I would've worked for free.

Me on the left side
her on the right.
Tried to get her grinning
but she was tight.

I said *I'm not like*
She said *Heard that before*
I said *I swear I*
She said *Heard that before.*

Walking toward the lockers
she offered me a smoke.
I smiled when she lit it.
She said *What's the joke?*

I guess I'm like the others
blowing smoke in her face.
I've seen the foreman grab her—
he's always on her case.

But I love that woman, I tell Odie.
He says, *No room for love in here.*
It's not just her looks, I tell him.
He says *C'mon, let's grab a beer.*

And we punch out, wash the grease
off our hands, step out the gate
where the fresh air beats
beats against my face. Her face.

WORK SONG: FACTORY MUSICAL

The whole line broke down
so we was all standing round
when Spooner picked up
two welding sticks
and started banging away
on an axle housing
playing that factory beat—
all of us gathered round,
it was a Friday.

Clapping hands
and old Paul P.
plump and slow in coveralls
tapping one foot
and then the other
shaking and dancing
round and round
and singing a song
in another tongue.

Nita started a disco dance
and Odie dancing hoedown style
and we was hopping and bopping
all down aisle C
when Santino came
but laughed and shrugged
and clapped in time
with the factory beat—
just drums no horns no strings just
boompa tappa boompa tappa

then our man Spooner twirled around
tappa tappa on the floor
boompa boompa on machine
and on the welding helmet of old Paul P.
like Hollywood

and we all dancing shouting
Go go gooooo!
and even Old Green
ready to retire
managed to smile his dance

we all so proud and flaunting
sweating, the music pounding inside
'til all the sudden
it was time
to return to the line.

3

DIGGER

DIGGER DRIVES TO WORK

The morning paperboy
tire groaning against fender
grass plastic with frost.
A car backs out of a driveway.
A car backs out of a driveway.
A car backs out of a driveway.
Gates close. Dogs out.
From fence to fence to fence
the same dog's face
steamy breath rising
through the mesh.

In the rearview mirror
the same grim face
in the car behind you
puffing a cigarette
looking at a watch.
You check yours:
you will be on time again.

An accident on the freeway.
You crawl past the flashing lights
bitching about the tie-up.
A cop waves you past.
You nod your head
moving with the flow
until you see a shoe on the road.
A corpse with one shoe.
You look at your feet on the pedals
for a half second:
work shoes. Check watch.
Your heart stutters.

The song changes
and you nod your head again.
But the sirens. Suddenly you notice
the sirens. You turn up the radio.

■■

Your car speeds up as traffic thins.
You look at your watch.
Maybe you will be late
after all. With one hand you open
your cold black lunch bucket:
bologna again.
You lick the mustard off your fingers.

DIGGER GOES HUNTING

When fall starts chilling into winter
you grab your rifle and drive north
with a couple buddies from the plant.

You stagger through the woods
whiskey heavy and whiskey warm
startling every animal for miles
with your song. You doze
against a tree until

a big creature crashes toward you
through the woods. You pull
your gun to your shoulder
and shoot twice. The animal falls.

You stand over a young doe.
You have no permit
so you find a shovel to bury it
chipping at hard earth
sweating whiskey.

The next day padding sober
down a trail you feel that doe's heart
beating under your feet. Branches
fill your head, and you suddenly fear
everything alive and moving
in these woods.

You clutch your gun tighter.
and move on. You've trusted steel
too long to stop now.

DIGGER GOES ON VACATION

The maps from AAA, the tour books—
you are well prepared:
Florida here we come.
For the first time your son
will not go with you.
He has a legit excuse:
a job at the corner store.
It is only you and the girls.
You think of your wife
as a girl. You think
that you have given her nothing.
At the first Stuckey's on the road
you buy her a box of peanut brittle
and smile weakly as she kisses
your cheek. Then you think
of the plant—she is kissing you
goodbye in the morning.
You feel a chill. Maybe wind
on your neck. You have
two weeks. Your body shakes
as you pull back on the road:
you have fifteen more years.

■

First night you stop
at a motel off I-75 in Kentucky.
You eat a late dinner in the coffee shop,
the girls nodding off to sleep
in their burgers. You look
at your wife Loretta. If somehow
she could lose some weight.
Then you look at your own belly
hanging over your belt:
but mine's hard, you tell yourself,
muscle. You punch your gut:
if we could just lose all this weight.

"Digger?"
"Oh. Yeah."
You pay the bill
and walk back to your room
squeezing Loretta's hand
like a snowball you want to melt.

■■

You lie in the sand,
the sun crisp on your back.
You'll get burned.
You always do.
You try to read a book
in the bright glare—the same
book from last year: *The Godfather*.
At a cabin in northern Michigan
you read a hundred pages
and killed mosquitoes.

She packed it to keep me busy,
keep my eyes off the women.
You look over at Loretta
in her floppy sun hat, bulging out
from her bathing suit. You toss sand
on her belly: "hey Loretta, gimme
a beer." She hands you one
from the cooler by her side.

She really does care about me,
you think, and suddenly you smile
and put the cold beer against her neck
and she jumps up screaming.
"Hey baby, I love you."
"What?" She takes off her sunglasses
and laughs, hugging you.
"You haven't said that
since . . . last year's vacation!"

You stare out at the sea of skin
and wonder when you'll say it again.

■

At the beach, your foot
in the sand outlines the part
you weld onto axles.

"What's that, daddy?"
You kick sand over the drawing.
"Nothin'." But no matter
how many times you kick the sand
it still looks like something.

■

In a motel in Tennessee
you peel off your skin
to gross your daughters out.
"Oh Daddy, that's sick!"
You laugh and rub your vacation beard:
"When all this skin is gone,
I'll be a new person."
"Who will you be then, Daddy?"
"I'll be an astronaut
so I could get lost in space."
"You're already lost in space,"
Loretta shouts from the bathroom.

That night after dinner
you drink alone at a local bar.
Your hands hold up your head
like obedient stilts. This is how
you always become a new person.
You talk to the bartender:
"I used to be an astronaut."
And he believes you.

DIGGER TIES ONE ON

Foreman writes you up
for sleeping on the job.
You lose a buck in the change machine
and twenty at lunch poker.

Your kid's suspended from school.
Drugs, and Loretta blames you
for ignoring him.

In the locker room, changing
into street clothes, you decide
to erase.

■■

After downing a few at Bruno's
you think about calling home
but your hands won't hold anything
smaller than a shot glass
so you keep throwing dollars
at Rachelle behind the bar.
She keeps the change.

Tomorrow with a fat head
of guilt and fuzzy pain
won't be any better.
You read every joke
on the bar napkin
without a smile.
No Fun you write
in a puddle of beer.

You know what's next:
coffee, the quiet ride home.
You have your choice of stories.
All beginning with *mistake*.

Rachelle kids you:
"Diggin' your grave tonight,
eh Digger?"
You open your eyes:
"Another inch or two."

DIGGER'S TERRITORY

Some would say
there's not much to
a life lived on your street.
They might say you're dumb
you watch too much TV
you drink too much
fart and belch and laugh too loud
dress funny and eat too many burgers.

But tonight after work
after you wash your hands
eat a good meal
wrestle with the dog a little
after you grab a beer
and sit on your porch
with your family, sharing a laugh
with a couple neighbors
while the sun sets behind
the bowling alley, after a man parks
his car carefully behind
your Impala up on blocks
and walks stiff up your driveway
in his suit and briefcase and perfect hair
and holds out a soft hand,
you all smile at each other
because no matter what he knows
you're going to teach him
a few things.

DIGGER ON THE NATURE TRAIL

You don't know much
about the natural world.
In high school you had print shop,
electronics, power mechanics, auto shop,
and outdoor chef, though no one
believes that one.

They were preparing you
for the life of your parents
but then everything became fuel injection
and they took all the fun
out of tuning up a car.

When you were a kid
the robots in the cartoons were evil.
They did not do what they were
supposed to do. Now they've got robots
who *do* what they're supposed to,
and that's the true evil.

It's like they ripped your name tag
off your forehead and it was taped on
with some kind of super ultra duct tape
that ripped the skin off too. You used to think
it was duck tape.

Now you've got time to take walks
and notice things. You drive out
to the county park some sunny mornings
when looking for work seems like a crime.

You were raised on the TV box
flashing its dreams like candy.
And it was good enough just to see
the candy. You didn't have to taste it.

You hadn't read a book in years,
but you've got one on birds now—
lots of pictures—and you compare
what you see to the pictures.
It's like filling in some big crossword puzzle.
That's what you used to do to help you sleep
when you had a job.

For a guy who didn't read, you did pretty good.
Learned all those words you only find
in puzzles, checking your answers
the next day. You had to have a system
just like at your old job. How to double-up
and cheat the clock.

No cheating the clock now,
with its slow lazy hours circling
while you wander the nature trail
thinking, *That's a pretty bird.*
I wonder what it's called.

You've got binoculars, the works.
Guys from work would be laughing
their asses off if they saw you out there.
Where are they all now? Not on the nature trail.

You're going to have to do something
about money soon. You got an A in outdoor chef,
but so did everybody else. Maybe that means
your school had the best goddamn burger cooks
in the world, but you think it means something else.

Running out of birds here. You dream about going
down to Florida—the Everglades—a lot of pretty birds
down there. And maybe a job. You were
a good tune-up man. Didn't need computers.

You could hear things under the hood of a car—
the voice of your dead grandpa, you swear,
telling you what to do.

Lately, he's been telling you to quit feeling sorry
for yourself. *Get on with it,* he's been saying.
It's like when Detroit went from being
the stove capitol to the car capitol—
your grandpa picked up on that and got a job
with "old Henry," as he called him—Henry Ford.

As if he ever met the man. Most people
don't remember that about Detroit, the thing
about making stoves. They used to have
The World's Largest Stove at the fairgrounds.
Now, they got a Giant Tire out near the airport.
What'll be next, you keep wondering.

They keep saying service jobs,
which means cooking burgers, for one thing.
Mr. Brand, your old football coach
who taught outdoor chef, he must be getting
a good laugh out of that—if he isn't dead.

You get dizzy a lot these days,
like you're suddenly aware of the world spinning.
Weekdays on the nature trail, you're usually
the only one. Once you saw a parakeet,
somebody's escaped pet. It made everything else
seem drab. Even your grandpa asked,
What's that pretty bird doing here?

DIGGER LAPS AT THE BOWL

The clock's dusty face on the wall
like yours, unshaven and silent.

Another hot one, the radio reports.
Vacation, and you're staying home.

The newspaper whispers on your lap
like a new map to someplace old.

Your wife is out. Out happily
with a list and a clutched set of keys.

You're supposed to be painting.

Once your credit-card number
ended up in China at a luxury hotel.

Once driving on bald tires with no spare
you got a flat near the Zilwaukee Bridge

and ruined two days of a camping trip.

Your favorite radio host died
last month—bad liver.

Thirty years of mornings, and his voice
gone, damn it, gone. A buyout's coming

and you'll have to take it or lose out
by retiring later. They're still trying out

new voices. This week is like practice,
imagining the clock's endless circle

without the breaks, the lunches,
the Fridays, the overtime, the cheating

minutes, the small satisfying thefts.
Today's radio voice is tinny and smartass.

You rise, cup your hands under the sink,
and fill them. Water trickles through

while you suck in what you can.

4

M-80

M-80

ROBERT KENNEDY SHOT. Early June
my mother prayed the rosary
in front of the hollow crucifix in her room
that slid open to reveal death candles
hidden for last rites' blessing.
They'd get used soon enough.

She prayed a long time. My father
wanted dinner. We ate mac and cheese.
Wipe your mouth
you've got that orange stuff all over it.
You're a big boy now—try to eat right.
A day when everything stuck to my face,
my 12th birthday. *Postponed,*
my mother whispered through tears.

■

Bobby. Bobby Kennedy, Debbie said,
balancing on the curb. She wore
a white blouse, shirttail out over cutoffs.
She drew a blue heart on her tennis shoe.
I wanted to fill it in.

What could we do
in the gray light of clouds
and broken glass, the stale wads
of gum clutching our teeth?
It was after a rain and we rode through puddles
it was a banana-seat stingray
it was one speed and one speed only.
She rode behind me on the seat
her thin legs swaying just above the ground.

We bought Twinkies and Orange Crushes.
I said *I have an orange crush on you.*
She laughed.

My birthday got rained out, I told her.
Assassinated. Our laughs short,
hollow. *Why does everybody
hate everybody?* Debbie asked.
Her parents had just split.
I don't hate you, I said.

Look at you, she said and put down
her Crush, licked the cream around my lips.
An M-80 went off in my chest—at least
it seemed that way. I'd bought five of them
from Artie Pilkowski, saving them for the 4th.
But I would use one soon enough
to blow up a mailbox—I was not immune.
Artie lost part of his hand that summer,
another of those hard-way lessons
we kept hearing about.

Behind the store we held each other and kissed
birthday kisses even after it was dark
even after it rained some more.

I kicked up my kickstand and rode her home
under the blue streetlights. She held on
tighter than I've ever been held.
My brother stood on the corner
smoking with his friends.
Junior's got a girlfriend, they said.
We were fierce and serious as I pedaled past.

My mother was praying again, and the TV was off.
I knelt beside her, my elbows sinking
into the soft bed, offering up
my small explosions.

CRAZY EDDIE

wasn't crazy. He was a drunk
garbage man with a bad temper.

He shot Porters' pigeons
for shitting on his garage.
The Porters, who had no kids
and gave us each a sucker
if we stood on their porch and sang
their name: *Porter, Porter-er*
like good little boys.

They dressed their dog Pee Wee
in tiny sweaters, gave him his own room.
They built a high stone wall
between their house and Eddie's.

He took our balls when they landed
in his yard. A pail of them
we saw through a basement window.

■■

In his bright white t-shirt
and green work pants,
in his greased-back hair
and beer gut, thick forearms
and squint and scowl,
he drenched his lawn in toxic fertilizers
while his two daughters played
alone on the sidewalk.

He set fire to the field
behind his house where we played ball.
Crazy, Crazy Eddie, we shouted, running
past his house, midnight.
Devil's Night he hid in the bushes
with a pellet gun. His cigarette glowed.

We didn't know then
he picked up trash for a living
and drank twelve beers a night.
Maybe all he wanted was a green lawn
and a peaceful drunk.

■■

Years later I worked in the beer store
where every day he brought his empties.
He said hello to me then,
and thank you. I handed him his change,
looked him in the eye. I'm the one
who burned *fuck you* into his lawn.

Maybe we just weren't smart enough
to know who to hate, a bucketful of balls
the only wealth we understood.
Hauling garbage all day, the stink
and mess of it. A perfect lawn.
What did we know, just a bunch of kids
learning that you had to sing
for your candy.

PARKED CAR

Fred and I, drunk and stoned,
drove around laughing like we did
in the old days before I met Karen.
Then I said *drive by Karen's*
and he said *are you sure?*
Then he said *okay* like he was tired
and didn't want to end up
bailing me out again.
She'd given my ring back a month ago.
I knew she had a date.

A car was parked
where I always parked.
Fred pulled in on the other side of the street.
We sat there. *There's no one in the car*
Fred said. No lights in the house.
I squinted hard through the dark,
saw a head pop up above the seat
then down again. I reached for the door.
There's no one in the car—
we're leaving now, Fred said.
He put his hand on my shoulder
gentle, firm.

⠿

I turned to stone then crumbled
wanting her and not wanting her
while Fred drove me home.
I held my open hand out the window
against the cold wind.

25 years ago.
Today in a moment rain
changes to snow.
Maybe it was Fred I loved that night.

We'd have never called it that.
And I still wouldn't to his face—
that small touch
during the years none of us
ever touched each other.

Sometimes I still drive by that spot
with my wife who doesn't know the ghosts
living there. We don't kiss in cars anymore.
Karen married, moved away.

Ah, heart. Hearts.
Mine and yours. Yeah, all of you.
The times we've given it away
for chump change.
The heart, the fist. If you're lucky
someone grabs your shoulder.

ANTHEM

Two months after retirement
my father is here, to get away
from 6 A.M. and his cup
of empty destination.

At a football game, we huddle
under his flimsy umbrella
talking about the obvious.
He brings me coffee
to hold warm between my hands,
a gift of no occasion.

When we rise for the anthem
I hear the rusty crack of his voice
for the first time maybe ever.

33 years of coughing
thick factory air, of drifting to sleep
through the heavy ring of machinery,
of 12-hour days. In my sleep
I felt the cold bump of his late-night kiss.

I shiver in the rain
as my father sings me
what now I hear as
a children's song. I lean
into him, the umbrella and rain
my excuse, my shoulder against his,
and I imagine my mother
falling in love.

TIME, TEMPERATURE

—for James Baldwin

1967, Detroit. My grandfather watches
tracer bullets zing past
his window. The National Guard's taken over
Lillibridge School on the corner.

> He remembers the strike at Packard
> when they promoted blacks,
> then the riots in '43,
> how the crowds gathered on Belle Isle
> just down the road, all the bloodshed
> just down the road.

On the phone with my father, he is saying *niggers*
and my father is saying *Dad* he is saying
Dad stay in the house, stay away from the window.

> My grandfather has his theories
> why they can't take the cold
> can't skate can't swim
> why they can't park their cars
> why grape's their favorite flavor
> why if you get bit by one with purple lips
> it will kill you.

My father shakes his head into thick air
saying *stay away, stay away.*
A drop of sweat hits the dirty kitchen floor.
Dad. Dad. My father's long sigh.

▪▪

Eenie, meanie, miney, moe
catch a nigger by the toe
our toes wedged in a tight circle
to see who'd be It. My mother
wouldn't let us say *nigger.*

She said say *froggy.*
We said *froggy.* The other kids said
froggy?

She washed my mouth with soap.
Where did you hear that word?
I heard it everywhere. *Where?*

■■

1967. 11, I climbed on the garage
with my father's camera. In the streaked photos
flocks of helicopters blotch the sky, nothing
like birds. I held on to the rough shingles
as the spinning blades roared above me.
Helicopters spilled guardsmen
onto the armory lawn on 8 Mile Road,
the border between Detroit and Warren.

We lived on that edge. Sirens
wailed their crazy tune, no Motown Sound,
nothing we could dance to.

Fear of heights seemed more real
than what I heard on the radio, than rumors
panting on the street: *They're at Belmont.*
They're at Farwell Field.
They're crossing 8 Mile.

Getting up was easy. I needed help
getting down, my feet dangling in air,
the camera somersaulting down onto the grass.

■■

8 Mile Road. 6 lanes wide. The long barbed
shout, pale slab, sizzling fuse.

I didn't know a black person 'til I was 19.
I could have almost shouted from my porch.

■■

Nigger pile. Riding nigger.
Nigger pile on Tony. Nigger beard.
Nigger stompers. Nigger-rigged.
Nigger-lipped. Niggered up. Nigger pillows.
How far you have to chase that nigger
to get that shirt? A fight, a fight
a nigger and a white.

Should I explain the terms, include an index
and glossary? Do we all possess
such footnotes, filed, hidden, backward,
in code, watermarks revealed by light?

Plenty of words for hate around here.
Like Eskimos with snow, we have
our subtle distinctions.

No one can trace
all the secret white tunnels
or break the white code.
Invisible, white on white.
Squint and hope for the best.

■■

1970. Roger Edwards, our new history teacher,
gave us roles to play: KKK members,
Black Panthers. I was Huey Newton.
I said *honky* and *pig* a lot.
I wore a black beret. We dressed in black,
took toy guns to class.

I learned a little about the burning fuse—
Bobby Seale, H. Rap Brown, Stokeley Carmichael.
If this town don't come around . . .

We knew our town hadn't, and how it burned.
Huey Newton walking into our class
would have turned us all to tin soldiers,
brittle glass.

Roger taught us what he could
till the nuns fired him.
He played records by Lightning Hopkins,
Coltrane, such strangeness we wanted to like
because he liked it. He let us swear in class
but he made us swear
not to say *nigger.*

■

Our fathers worked with their fathers
in factories in Detroit, Warren,
brought home their hate in greasy lunch pails:
Better watch out for that nigger.
That's a nigger department.
Don't help that nigger,
lazy nigger.

It spilled across the dinner tables,
through the muddy alleys,
across the concrete playgrounds,
into the schools, and we learned
our lessons well.

■

1974. Black students
from Pershing High two miles away
visited Fitzgerald, my school.
We asked them questions
in a room crowded with teachers
who prompted us in whispers.
So foreign even those translators couldn't help.

Stilted as a high-school play.
Someone took pictures for the yearbook.

They filled our halls with a flavor
foreign and pungent. Some new kind of cooking
I wasn't sure about.
The next day in class we sat glum
while a perky teacher preached brotherhood.
We knew better. *They only brought
the nice ones,* somebody said.

■■

1975. I worked in a liquor store
where we didn't cash checks for blacks
but sold them booze and cigarettes.

A man held a gun to my head
*where's your hiding place
where's your fuckin' hiding place?*
I said we don't have a hiding place
he said *motherfucker, everybody
got a hiding place*
I said we took it to the bank
he said *I'm gonna kill you motherfucker
where's your hiding place?*

His gun brushed my temple.
We looked each other in the eye: no recognition.
He grabbed money from the register,
took off down 8 Mile. I reached down
and clutched the cigarette carton
filled with checks and twenties.
The boss called the cops.
Fingerprints on a can of Colt 45
and no clues or suspects.
Colt 45, I said, *figures.*
I flipped through the mug shot pages:
Some nigger, I said.

■■

Carl the gun collector
handed out rifles to the neighbors
in '67 *just in case just in case*
they cross 8 Mile. To protect
our families and homes, he said.
The right to bear arms.
My father did not take one.

In 1974 under the threat of busing
neighbors took pledges
put signs in their windows:
I will not send my kids.
I will keep my kids home.
My mother took no sign.

The Supreme Court ruled against
cross-district busing.
Neighbors smiled archly
no thanks to you, as if my mother
was a scab in this union town.

■■

My grandparents both got mugged
on their street. My grandmother bent
into a sad turtle in her chair,
dazed and afraid, black circles
deep under her eyes in the house
her parents built.

We ate early when they came over
so they could be home before dark.
The golden rule: home before dark.

My grandfather would not move,
spraying his hose on the fire
in the abandoned house next door,

buying up the vacant lots around him
ten bucks a piece.

They watched their one good television
in a living room lined with three broken ones
so they won't know which one to take.

9000 vacant lots in their old neighborhood,
another 1000 homes empty, boarded up.

*There's only three things
wrong with blacks,* he said.
They lie, they steal, and they kill.
He did say *blacks.*

■■

My grandfather loaded up his old Ford
with stale cakes from Sanders,
bruised fruit and vegetables, to distribute
to the poor for Father Connors, the priest
from the church across the street.
St. Rose, razed now, just another vacant lot.

He fixed bikes for the black kids
on his street. Kids. Kids
were kids, the contradictions
rattling around his head,
as if he had separate brains
for theory and practice,
separate hearts.

Old man. All things harden inside him.
No way to explain generations
of prejudice, poverty, and hunger,
bad schools and no hope, and hate,
no way to explain it.

In Detroit, it has always been a matter
of taking sides. *They
drove us out of Detroit,* he says.

■■

My old neighborhood in Warren
red-lined. Too close to 8 Mile.
Blacks moving in. Property values
plunging. *Shoulda sold years ago,*
a realtor said.

Old neighbors move out, refining their excuses.
Two streets over, a black family lines the curb
with boulders to keep cars off their lawn.

■■

A black guy on the assembly line
offered to break my machine for me
accidentally. I nodded.
We stood together, not smiling
just breathing and waiting

waiting and resting
resting and sighing
sighing and nodding.

The nod. It's too easy
to say *That's the kind
of cooperation we need.
That's the kind of cooperation we need.*

■■

Dogs growl. Women peek out curtains.
A black man is delivering circulars
on a hot August afternoon in 1968
surrounded by the echo of his own steps.

He is coming up our walk.
My mother opens the door, offers him iced tea.
I sit on the stoop, staring.
My mother leans against the bricks.
I can hear his throat swallowing
the cold tea. Little
is said and what is said
is about the heat.
Thank you, he says. *Back to work.*

Hope your mom washed that glass good.
Something I will hear from time
to time. Not too loud
or too mean, but I will hear it.

■■

1980. In the department store,
those foam packing chips that last forever
poured from an overhead funnel
into gift boxes full of vases, clocks, books,
ceramic dogs, martini glasses, china, silver.
To cushion and protect.

Kim's dark skin
surrounded by the white, white foam.
We worked in that blizzard together.
We leaned across the table toward each other
in the basement under the store
where all the black people worked,
along with me and another white kid.

We felt like robots down there,
filling and sealing. Till our eyes locked
in the hard stare of mannequins.
We ate lunch together
in the lounge. People talked.
It only took me a year to ask her out.

Dixie scowled. *What are you doing?*
This is Detroit you're talking about.

We went to a movie in my part of town,
for coffee in her part.
I can't remember what we saw
because I held her hand in the dark
and we were alone there just like
two white kids, or two black kids.

All night the stares bit into us
like tiny bugs we couldn't see.
Walking to the car, I squeezed
her hand into a fist.
I guess you have to be rich
to get away with it, she said
and maybe she was right.

Our own sizzling skins could not
our own good fire could not blend
or overwhelm or distract or soothe enough.
We were not rich enough or fast enough, fat enough
or thick-and-thin enough. We could not slam
our car doors loud enough to break the long stare.

At work the next day
the foam rained down between us.
It lay in heaps.
I couldn't look at her.
I grabbed two handfuls and squeezed:
nothing can destroy them.

■■

I said *Some nigger robbed the store*
and the cop said *What else is new?*
Get a gun, he said.
The board tilts, and all the balls
roll into the same hole.

I felt bad, but I said it anyway.
My shrunken head, tiny eyes
sewn shut. There is no
immunization, no shot, no cure,
no pill, no magic, no saint,
no argument, no prophet,
no potion, no confession,
no gift, no miracle, no fucking miracle.

No.

■■

Last summer, the dog next door
scared away two black kids
trying to break into my basement.
I saw them running away. A week later
the same two kids cased out a house
down the street. I stood at the door
watching, sweating, heart jumping.

I stepped out toward them. They said
You keep following us you're gonna get hurt.
I said *I'm only trying to protect my property.*
They said *Listen man, you wanna get hurt?*

No, I don't want to get hurt.
Yes, I have property now,
an old house in this mixed neighborhood.
Maybe I was afraid because they were black.
Maybe they were angry because I was white.
I tried to talk calmly but I know enough
about being stoned to know
they were stoned on something.

Everybody stoned on something—
stoned on history and hate.

Everybody got a hiding place.

■

Pressed flat to the shingles
a little afraid of the height
as the helicopters pass
a little afraid of the noise and sirens
a little afraid of blacks
and rumors and everything I don't understand:
why burn, why here?

■

1990. Waiting for the light at 8 Mile and I-75
I see a naked black man lunge between cars,
two cops chasing him, his feet slapping
hot cement in the silence of engines idling July heat
two cops chasing him down the road
between Detroit and Warren
between two hard places,
and he is naked and soft and running
till the cops wrestle him to the ground
scraping his knees and chin.
I pass by as he lies there getting cuffed.
As he lies there.

He looks a little dazed. The cops lift him
by the cuffs and he stands, his arms
tight behind him. He looks a little stoned
a little stoned on something.
The cuffs cut into his wrists
but he barely flinches.
Even naked, he barely flinches.

Maybe his story is the story I want to tell.
But I do not know his story.

I do not know what he has done.
I am telling you everything I know.

■

Carl took his guns back
but they are there someplace.
I know Carl. His nose twitches
with the gunpowder of his own hate.

They are someplace.

■

I am trying to be naive.
It has come down to this.
Naive enough to keep from being rolled
into another bitter pill.

An open fire hydrant in hot August
after an afternoon game at Tiger Stadium.
I am walking toward my car.
A young black kid, maybe 6, is dancing
in his underwear in the cool spray
he is holding his wrists up toward the sky
as if to say *Take me, take me like this,*
and I am so hot I join him
dancing too in cut-offs and t-shirt

and I raise my arms above my head
thinking *yes, I would like to be taken like this*
and we dance under the same sun
and there is room enough for both of us
in the spray on Rosa Parks Boulevard
in Detroit in Michigan in America saying
take me take me under one big sun
that will take us, take us all,
in its own good time.

BROKE

I-75 near Livernois
my '68 Satellite dropped
its drive shaft.
I guzzled my beer
though I wanted to puke
thinking about the money
I didn't have.

I walked to a gas station
where a man with a gun
in his back pocket
got me a tow truck.

I gave the driver
one of my beers.
His chapped hands bled.
In the cold cab
smelling of french fries
and oil, I tried to joke
but he wasn't joking.
Halfway home I calculated
the cost of the tow
plus the drive shaft
was worth more than the car.

He dropped it in the street,
yellow lights circling over bricks.
Some people looking out
I could see. Despite the beer
he overcharged me.
Orange lights racing
caution through my gut,
my wallet entirely too thin.

He threatened to take the car
back to the garage till I paid
the rest. I waited him out.

We both knew the car
wasn't worth shit.
I had two beers left
and I gave him one.

After he drove away
I sat on the curb
pulling pieces of rust
out of the door. Tomorrow
I'd make the rounds of junkyards
looking for a drive shaft
with my sincerity and bad check.

That week I'd applied for jobs
as a janitor, busboy, ice cream man.
I was hoping for the ice cream job—
a little joy behind the wheel
a little white truck
bells ringing through clean suburbs.

I made a little tower of rust
on the manhole cover.
Everything seemed that fragile.
I'd clamped a tin can on my exhaust pipe
to hold it together. A bean can.

Sucking on the tailpipe
taking a deep sleep:
that rusty thought gnawed me
while I sat next to the car
going no place.

I'd like to play it down,
that melodramatic night.
It's like when you see the flashers
and think it's the cops or an ambulance
but it's only a tow truck
hauling away another junker.

A few months later I got a decent job
but drove that old car longer than I had to,
held onto it like a nubby candle,
afraid getting rid of it
would jinx my luck. I had to lie
a little to get the job
but like the bean can
it was just another stretch.

I got a hundred for it
because it started and ran.
Sold it to a man who knew
all about tin cans.
We shook hands in the street.
I gave him the block of wood
I used to hold the heater vent open,
a little something solid, a little gift.

TROUBLE AT THE DRIVE-IN

The sky is gray and it will be
raining soon and we're waiting in line
for the drive-in, the one on 8 Mile,
the border between Detroit and Warren and the anger
is stewing just like always, every day
guns pointed at our own dumb heads, every day
somebody else dumb enough to pull the trigger
because we're mad, mad and sick and dumb
and we're gonna get ourselves a little piece of something
even if it means taking it away from someone else
who don't have much, or else we're sick and tired
of everybody taking like that, so we're gonna
protect ourselves, by God, though God
don't seem to help much here—He's getting ripped
off too—and we all want to have our say
one way or another, so there's a lot of guns
in a lot of hands, yes, I'm thinking all this here
as it starts to pour, fucking rain like crazy,
and I say *fuck* to let you know I mean
business, just like why I carry a gun,
so it's fucking raining and if you don't like it
then fucking get lost because I'm still going
to the movies—a Clint tripleheader—
Fistful, A Few Dollars More, and *Good/Bad/Ugly,*
and all these good, bad, ugly people are leaning
on their horns and some asshole cuts his car into the line
up front and this big fat guy gets out of his car and runs
up to that car and he's screaming *fuck you*
so he means business, and he's pounding on the windows
yanking on the door, and he's getting soaked,
but he don't give a fuck, he is me and he is you,
and the guy in the car is me and you
and we're all kicking each other's asses
while the bosses are safe and dry
in Grosse Pointe or West Bloomfield or wherever
the fuck they live, laughing at *New Yorker* cartoons

and thinking Woody fucking Allen is a genius, let me
tell you, Clint ain't no genius, but I understand
his movies, and I understand what's going on
up ahead, and I'm hearing sirens, and me and you,
we're in this together, buddy, just a couple dummies
like those two up there, and nobody's letting us in
and nobody's getting out, and it's only a matter of time
till somebody pulls a gun.

5 NIAGARA FALLS

NIAGARA FALLS

"Brother Leo, to be a saint means to renounce not only everything
earthly but also everything divine."

—St. Francis of Assisi, in *Saint Francis,* by Nikos Kazantzakis

My wife and I eat cold spaghetti,
overpriced, after waiting all night
for it in a restaurant called Mama Something's.

I study the tip chart I keep in my wallet,
the stares of Mama's boys
like loaded guns. I leave more
than I want, and hurry out
into the clear autumn night
so I can breathe again.

I can afford this bad meal
and our hotel room in Niagara Falls.
Some people think I'm cheap,
the way I can't relax
about money, counting it,
making sure. I envy the easy grace
of credit card and *keep the change.*
My parents never stayed in hotels
or went out to eat.
We stayed at home. At home, we ate.

All night I pop antacids.
I should've known better
than to eat in a restaurant
called Mama Anything's.

▋▋

25 years ago, here,
on a rainy camping trip
my father splurged on
Ripley's Believe It
Or Not Museum where I stared

at the shrunken head.
I bought a postcard:
The Hair continues to grow.
I still have it: long beaded threads
hang from the nose like a rosary.

25 years ago, in a Detroit church
that's now a gym, I took St. Francis
as my confirmation saint
though Francis was a sissy name.
He talked to animals,
hung out in the woods—
Brother Sun, Sister Moon.

I took that name
and my parents gave me my first watch.
Its band pinched my wrist—
I wasn't ready for that kind of time,
that kind of skeptical attention.

■■

A chart in school kept track
of our memorized prayers. I have forgotten
them all, though I know the beginnings,
little snatches. With a prompter
I could probably make it through.

The Act of Faith, Act of Hope, Act
of Love. The Act of Contrition,
the only one I remember—
". . . and lead us not into temptation . . ."
The Act of Constriction.

■■

25 years ago, a fat blustering priest
was suffocating me. Lost
in his thick black robes
I slit my way open to the light.

The other priest smoked pot,
listened to rock, married my classmate,
disappeared. Showed up years later,
singing in the choir.

I haven't been to church in years.
I pray at the Shrine
of the Shrunken Head. I recite
a cautionary tale, a prayer
for a good life, a prayer
for my shrinking head,
my shrinking heart,
a prayer against
my own disappearance.

Halo, halo, who's got the halo?

■■

We pay to ride an elevator up a tower
overlooking the Falls. Foggy,
nothing to see. We take our time
staring into the wet gray air,
getting our money's worth.

When we're ready to descend,
the elevator won't come—
the line winds around the tiny deck
like a curled whip.

■■

After I wrote about giving up on God
my history teacher had me read
Dostoevsky's *The Grand Inquisitor*
and Russell's *Why I Am Not a Christian.*

I called myself an agnostic
and blessed myself with sweet smoke, cold beer.
I believed in cynicism. I developed

a first-class sneer. I became a first-class relic
of a good Catholic boy, cassock and surplice
too short, wrinkled, dusty on the closet floor.

■■

Francis the Talking Mule
was the only Francis I ever really knew,
in those old movies with Donald O'Connor,
the forerunner to Mr. Ed, the Talking Horse.
I could sing you Mr. Ed's song with no prompting:
A horse is a horse of course of course . . .
What it does for my spirit
I cannot tell you.

I once sent to Hollywood for an autographed
picture of Arnold Ziffel, the pig from *Green Acres*.
More of a piglet. Arnold only grunted
but his owner, Fred, understood Pig—
I like that kind of faith.
Mr. Ed was someone's voice,
no miracle: *Oh, Wilbur.* Francis
would not have understood you.

■■

Last year we lived in Torre Gentile,
a small village a short ride from Assisi.
I had to find out more about
the only name I had ever chosen.
What moved me in Assisi was Cimabue's St. Francis,
not the saintly one in Giotto's frescoes
where he looks too holy and wise to touch,
a religious superman lifting buildings,
casting out demons.

Cimabue's Francis would get his ass kicked
in the gym class locker room. Frail, homely,
big ears. They might call him that—Big Ears,
Dumbo. But he wouldn't be fun to tease—too quiet.

He wouldn't get mad. Maybe he'd even flunk gym
for refusing to box. The kind of kid
you wouldn't mind having sit across
from you in homeroom. He'd give a comfort
you'd be embarrassed by. *But he's a nice kid,*
you'd say, almost apologetically,
when someone called him a sissy.

■■

My oldest friend, Joe, goes to church again
and lifts weights.

His child was born deaf, deformed.
The church helps carry him through.
That, and the weights. He's almost deformed
with muscle, weightlifting magazines
scattered across his basement floor.

I have always been thin
like Joe used to be, though I tried
to gain, to be more substantial—
less wind-blown—more rooted
to the dusty earth.

■■

We were altar boys together
till we quit and started going out to eat
at the Clock Pancake House—
Our Lady of the Clock, our first
restaurant. We spent our paper route money.
It was our Mama Anything's.
We didn't know enough then
to read the fine print.

Those pancakes lay heavy in our guts
the sickening sweet syrup
sticking to our fingers.

■■

A rosary from the Assisi gift shop
won't heal anyone, Joe, nor will the muscles
you've built up. But maybe they will bring
a little peace, clear peace with no interference,
no background noise. A little peace here, now,
like when we walked through the winter dark
to serve at morning mass, the streets
quiet, headlights sifting through falling snow.

Maybe we could've simply turned around
and walked home then, blessed by the walk,
blessed by the holy frozen waters,
the snow falling on us,
without going in to the cruets and chalice,
our memorized prayers and stiff knees.

■■

A little peace, a good thing. A little
humility, the last word of Francis's prayer,
"Canticle of the Creatures." It moves me—
how else to say it?

Joe, what can we give each other but solace?
Here, let me offer up a dark snowy morning
before the world wakes up.

■■

I have been to Rome and seen a lock
        of John Keats's hair
but I have not been to Graceland
        nor to the Niagara Falls Elvis Museum
that maybe has a white suit similar to the one
        worn and sweated into and farted into
by the King himself. The King Himself. Exactly
        similar. A Mama's Boy, a Mama Anything's Boy.

Elvis, sing me a Canticle of the Blues
     sing me the blues
like on the old, scratched Sun Records
     before Mama took over.
Sing like a black man
     like a carp in murky water.
Elvis, you didn't die young enough
     to be a saint.

How many Cadillacs did Elvis really
     give away? If we unseal the lips
of the Shrunken Head will it sing
     "Love Me Tender"? Or
O bless and praise my Lord all creatures?

■■

I bought my ticket to the top, and I want down.

     We're all patient enough
cows waiting on that stuffy observation deck
     till we find out why the elevators won't come:
they're taking down the diners
     from the expensive restaurant one floor up.

After an hour we've observed enough
     at the top of the world.
We are the poor relations stuck
     at the card table in the kitchen.

A woman I will call St. Joan
     I know she has not been beatified
     let me be the first witness
says follow me
     and we do
     at least a hundred of us
up the staircase to the restaurant
     where we crowd among the wealthy diners
circle the dessert table, hold the bathrooms
     hostage. *Free drinks for everyone*

St. Joan says. The maitre d' grabs
  the phone, calls up that elevator
fast. He yells at us, but the edge of fear
  cracks his voice.

He could have intimidated each of us
  individually. Together
we snake among the tables, wiggling
  patting each other on the back.
No moo cows. No more passive milk.

■■

  I didn't go to worship Keats,
but I wanted to see his handwriting, his relics.
  Poor John Keats dying so young
he still thought he could be famous
  without Mama's help.
Keats's hair, Elvis's suit, Francis's implements
  of self-mortification, his simple robe and sandals.
Why do we worship where we do?
  I don't want to die. Have I told you that?
Vaya con Dios. Gimme that old time static
  it's good enough for me.

■■

St. Francis's simple old tunic
  under glass like it's an Elvis suit.
All I can do is smudge the glass
  when I want to break it
I want to touch the hem of his garment.
I want to touch it
                not wear it.

The signs asked for *silencio*
  but the tourists' gold bracelets
still clicked together.

■■

Outside the cathedral at Assisi
you can buy obscene carvings
    of drunken monks eating and drinking.
You can buy a battleaxe, Mama's stamp on the bottom
    that says "Authentic Fake."
You can buy St. Francis in all his famous poses.
    His "All Shook Up," his "Hound Dog."

Elvis has no stigmata but he has been seen
    eating hamburgers in Kalamazoo
ten years after his death. Listen to him chew.
    I have not bought any indulgences
though in grade school we bought
    pagan babies with our extra pennies.

■■

When the doors slide open
we file on, almost with regret,
slow and kind to each other,
willing now to wait.

It's just a moment. Maybe not enough
to make a saint. I'm no authority
but it's the kind of miracle
I believe in.

Back on the ground
we hold up our fists in the power sign,
surprised to find we'd paid our dues
in the same club, no coin in the fist,
just a pebble of the blues.

■■

Even half the Franciscans didn't believe
in that triple-decker sandwich

of a church in Assisi,
that Big Mac tribute to a simple man.

Thing is, it's beautiful.

In Detroit they built our new church
out of exposed cement, stained glass
in earth tones, someone's idea
of humility, like a parking garage
or the basement of an office building.
Whose idea? Francis's?

Why do we need a building
to worship in? Why don't we turn them
all into gyms? And yet, and yet,
why not worship beauty?
If you're gonna make a church
make it a goddamn beautiful one
so even folks like me who don't believe
can feel pretty damn inspired
by something? Hey Francis,
help me out here, will ya?

■■

A good meal at decent prices,
	a clean room with a big bed, yes,
they can give a little peace too.
I can afford it
	so what's the problem?
Do I feel I don't deserve it
	or that it's wrong to have it?
Wrong when the worn patched tunic
	not under glass is worn
and sweated in and shit in
	on the streets of our cities?

If Elvis got popsicle stains
	on his white suit, what's the problem?
Mama's stain remover gets those surfaces clean.

But clean surfaces weren't enough
for the King, and the kind of peace
    pills bought, the sleep
of the stunned cow, brought
    no waking solace.

■■

We ride the *Maid of the Mist* and take
color pictures of each other
to match the honeymoon black-and-whites
my parents took. They loved each other
in those pictures in a way I want us
to love each other. My parents
so young and beautiful it breaks my heart,
all the hard years ahead of them, five kids,
my father's long overtime years
in Mama's noodle factory
that twisted him, shook him out to dry
numb in his padded chair,
hissing out slow leaks,
ready to be numbed again
in front of the TV, wisps of smoke
from his cigarette trailing off.

My mother's disease
makes her dizzy all the time,
barely able to move some days.
She closed her eyes while we spun
in front of her, wild tops,
hungry tops.

■■

My parents could never afford our Italy trip,
38 years after their *Maid of the Mist*.
I asked my mother to pray
for us when we left.

She says a rosary every night—
at least one through her pain and worry
and lack of sleep. Comfort. Solace.

Dizzy all the time, that's what it is.
Shrunken head, that's what it is.
Funny how on top of the tower
our vertigo went away.

■■

St. Francis, your old man was rich.
You gave him back his fancy robes,
and he cut you out. I liked that part—
giving it all away, breaking
from the expected, shaking things up.
You were born Giovanni de Bernardone.
Frank—I will call you that.
Joan—I will call you that. Sainthood
screwed up the church, the worship of bones,
the selling of bones, the secret maps,
the big everlasting treasure.

It's this earth you praised, Frank.
Don't deny it.

■■

The Pope, Mr. His Holiness, JP2, reminds me
of recent American presidents.
Maybe that's just the nature of politics—
phony piety, like my altar-boy face
that brought more money
in the envelope after weddings, more money
to spend at Dairy Queen on the way home,
Mama's Soft Serve, where Joe and I got our first jobs
where the boss watered down everything
stuck his hairy arms in the ice cream vats
searching for a dropped quarter.

Maybe JP2 just eats too many meals
at Mama's table. It doesn't take too many meals
at Mama's table for the mask to form, all the juices
and sticky substances, how many times
have we seen it happen? He bends
to kiss the ground at airports,
but I have never seen him with dirt on his lips.
How does he do it? Brother Wind? Sister Water?
The JP2 World Tour, the Office of Papal Souvenirs,
the roadies, the groupies, the Pope-on-a-rope
rope-a-dope thrilla-in-Manila Magilla Gorilla
lunch box and nail-polish remover.

Step by step, inch by inch,
can I come back to you, Frank,
and leave the rest of it?

■■

On our way home the next day
through autumn's bright dying,
we stop at Pymatuning Spillway
off the narrow road where the carp gather—
carp so thick you could walk across them
and it wouldn't be a miracle, which is what,
miraculously, the ducks do.

We buy three loaves of stale bread for a dollar
and toss the pieces. We are practicing
being Mama Anything and it feels pretty good
to be the one tossing the bread. The carp
with their huge sucking frenzied mouths
open and swallow. It disappears instantly.
The monstrous sucking noises, the dancing ducks.
We can never get enough bread,
we will never be satisfied, we will never say
no, uh-uh, I've had enough.
Bread, what bread? Quit carping.

■■

The spillway is man-made, constructed
for the express purpose of giving
your average Joe the power of Mama—
briefly, the power of Mama.
How does one carp get so much bigger
than the others? If we threw money,
they'd swallow that too. We are throwing money.
Some of them want it more. They've got the Elvis gene,
they are descendants of the first Elvis, the biblical Elvis
who was slain by his brother Jerry Lee for his amazing
dream coat, his amazing dream Cadillac,
who was St. Francis's brother and took his song
the other way, the anti-Frank, managed by Pontius Pilate,
who lost a paternity suit to Mary Magdalene,
who raped Sam Cooke's mother,
who went up to the mountain and came back with a gold record,
who was elected a saint until they had a recount,
who was elected a martyr until it was discovered
he was really St. Paul and had never died at all.

■■

These Pymatuning pictures must be labeled
with a parental advisory. They have been condemned
by the Church. Please put black lines
through all the open mouths.
No true love here. No wonder of the world here.
I am Mama Anything
until the bread runs out. The greed,
the devouring. I get a hard on for it.
Draw a black line through the mouths,
keep them decent.

■■

I threw my last loaf all at once, the white pieces
fluttering down like enormous hosts, disappearing
in the chaos, the swarm, the swirl and splash,

the wailing saxophones of the seraphim, the cherubim,
the angelic orders, the dancing Satan doing the Funky Broadway
on the backs of the squirming Carp Girls
in their skimpy outfits, their big pouting mouths.

I can't get no.
I can't get no.

I try.
I try.

■

How long can one person stand
to throw the bread and watch?
The record is held by a woman from Tucson, Arizona,
by way of Truth or Consequences, New Mexico.
Mrs. Alva Rhubarb fed the ducks for 30 days and 30 nights
'til she passed out, 'til she won the radio-station prize
'til she had a vision and told the reporters
Just call me Mama.
        Mama what?
Mama Anything.

■

See, the thing is they not eatin'
nobody's body and blood.
They eatin' they own body and blood.
They own, get it?

Lemme look at that prayer again.

Frank, tell me about the stima-tata?
What's that sheeut all about?
Things got all fucked up
    when you got too many brothers signing up.
Things always get fucked up
    when you got too many brothers.

Frank, what about St. Claire, man?
What about the flesh? How come
that sister ain't in the prayer?

■■

When we got close enough to the Falls
to feel the spray, the boat turned around.
We'd gotten our money's worth.
We took off our black raincoats
full of the stink of hundreds of bodies,
of my parents' bodies and my wife's parents' bodies.
The stink of human flesh.

Pilgrims, that word comes to me.
Which implies journey, which implies faith.

■■

In a painting in a church in Spoleto
St. Agatha and St. Lucy
make their offerings to God.
One with her breasts on a plate,
the other, her eyes.

They think they are presenting their body parts
as gifts to God, but I think it is Mama
behind the altar, drooling and laughing,
napkin tucked around her neck.

St. Agatha, St. Lucy.
Their names floated by me
in the dark thin air of the church.
I whispered them. I wrapped
my arms around myself.

■■

My head shrinks a little every day.
My body shrinks a little every day,
Sister Bodily Death.

I pray along the beads of the shrunken head—
the head, my crucifix, my fear,
my final prayer, my death mask:
Hey, don't let me die,
amen, amen, amen.

Lifting weights won't keep me from shrinking.
My right muscle is bigger than my left.
I contradict myself because of the imbalance.
Pass the collection plate
for my left muscle.

■■

From Assisi we drove to Perugia
and bought ice cream from a Mama's Boy
who tried to shortchange me.

Yet, when we were leaving another store,
a man ran out to hand me the camera we'd forgotten.
We went back in and bought an assortment
of Perugina chocolates to reward the good deed
with international currency.

We ate them in the car.
They were wonderful—I won't deny it.
The things of the world are sweet
and the animals will not listen to us.
They know we speak with a foreign tongue.
They know we will kill them.

■

Maybe it's the moment
when the bread is in the air, that brief moment
when it's everyone's bread, before it touches down.

Everyone likes peace, but turn it
into a loaf of bread and see what happens.

■

As far as impersonators go
Elvis's got the lead.
Though people claim
to be Jesus Christ,
few make a living at it.
I don't know anyone, Frank,
anyone who claims to be you.

■

Francisco de Zurbaran
painted *St. Francis in Meditation*
with the saint kneeling in shadow,
just a little light on one shoulder,
the famous torn robe.
It never hits him directly.
He holds a skull in his praying hands.

His eyes raised, his mouth hanging open,
his face hollow as the skull.
The cord from his robe
dangles on the floor, long enough
to hang him.

I look closely
for the stigmata on his hands.
It is not visible.
No halo either.

Francisco, Francis, Frank.
Is that you?

■

The halo, the sign—
because you cannot tell a saint
on the street,
because you cannot tell a saint
in the church,
because you cannot tell
a saint without a scorecard,
because you cannot tell.

I would like to touch a halo,
the perfect arc, golden.
I bet it would warm my cold hands
with the solace of its glow.

■

My good friend Frank
is no saint,
as he would readily admit.
But he has his angelic moments.
I want to believe we all have angelic moments,
but I have come to believe
there are men without hearts
saying mass in the church
of Mama Anything.

In Assisi with Frank
we climbed to the hermitage above the town
where we breathed in the silence
St. Francis breathed.
We sat on rocks and did not speak.

How can we be good people
in this life?

Mother Earth.
Quiet, I can't hear her.
Mama, turn down the fucking jukebox.

■

Cimabue and de Zurbaran.
I have held postcards of those paintings,
one in each hand. They don't look
anything like each other
except for the robe.
One haunted, one at peace.

If the kid sitting across from you in homeroom
gets beat up in gym class every day
for a week or two, what happens to his spirit?

I am haunted and at peace.

■

Niagara Falls.
Step by step, inch by inch.
I'll take all that free water falling anytime.
All that free romance, anytime.
Sister Water . . . precious and pure.

Why do we want to go over
in a barrel? Why do we want
to go up in the tower?

Moe, Larry, Curly, come on out here
you crazy stooges. Let's give them
a big round of applause,
our hands slapping together,
our mouths gaping open.

I want to be saved. I am going over.
I can't help myself.

■

We are almost home, driving
in the chill of this autumn evening,
the sky so gray that darkness
will be a relief, headlights
will be a relief. My wife
sleeps softly against my shoulder
exhausted by bread
and the long numb hours
of our broken radio.
I hear a siren, but she does not stir.
I make the sign of the cross—
something I'd never let her see me do.

It is how I was taught, and though I know
it won't do a bit of good
for whoever's in the back of that ambulance
I want to at least signal the air, signal
my four corners
and this darkening world:
we are human and we're going to die.

I say to the person lying prone
zooming past: I am sorry
and I hope it's not now.

I say to the dead raccoon
by the side of the road:
we're in this together
though I know you don't believe me.

It is true that
no living man can flee
Sister Bodily Death.
But I am singing this song
to keep her away.

But I too will tire, and sleep.

■

We are carp swimming up river, Mama,
all of us, even you. I grip the steering wheel
in one hand. The other rests
on my wife's knee. My wallet against my ass
tells me little about who I am.
It is the prayer book the world insists on.
The tires hiss in my ears
like rushing water.

If I was a saint, I might
scoop out my dashboard full of change
and toss it to the wind.
But I am counting it out
to pay our toll.

6

BLESSING THE HOUSE

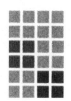

BLESSING THE HOUSE

I step out of the car and stare
at the flat houses with their bristly bushes
wild and short like my old hair.
I want to cut my hair and spread it over this snowy yard
like my own ashes, I want to curl inside a sidewalk square,
my ear to the ground, cupped, listening—what could I bring
back to life? Would I hear the rough chalk scrawl over cement?

This house the priest blessed over thirty years ago
when the lawn was mud and boards. *Bless this house,*
I think, standing in the street. The wind blows cold
but I know this wind, its harsh front.
Don't try to bully me, I say. I am home
and my hands are trembling, I am sighing.
The car door slams. I clap my hands
for the hell of it, a clap on a street corner
echoing a little, among friends.

Once I stood here for hours
trying to hit the streetlight with a snowball,
to leave a white smudge. I have left no smudge,
nothing I could call mine. The gray sky presses
down on these small houses, on my parents' house
and its square slab. They are inside,
maybe changing the channel on the TV, maybe
grabbing a beer and a bowl of chips, maybe
flushing the toilet, maybe scrubbing their faces,
maybe peering out a dark window.

I am waiting to step inside for the hug and the kiss,
I am waiting to push away this gray sadness—cement and sky.
I grab a handful of snow and touch it to my forehead
where it melts down my face. I smudge my chest
with an X of snow, I toss handfuls on the yard,
on the scraped sidewalk—ashes, ashes, glowing
in the streetlight before the melting, the disappearing.

Oh glorious snow, I say, *we have missed each other.*
I listen for a moment. I lift my bags from the trunk.
The porch light glows its yellow basket
of tender light. I stomp my boots, and I go in.

BIRCH BARK

I was the boy who wrote his name
on a piece of birch bark
and carried it home from Tea Lake
where my family spent a week
and I hid from everyone, lurking
on the edge of photographs.

I would like that week back—
a week my father wasn't working.
I couldn't let him inside me
only to give him up again
to the weary tie, the weary sigh
the morning glimpses through
his coffee and cigarette,
the lingering smells of shaving cream
and hair tonic as I brushed my teeth.

The peculiar child, I hid
while the others soaked him up,
fishing, swimming, clutching his pale skin.
His laugh, released from its cage,
echoed across the water to where I crouched
in the woods, gulping tears.

∷

He took me fishing, trapped me,
his air filling the rowboat
while I slumped in the bow, worried
I would catch it again and never get well.
I squirmed till he reached forward
and tickled me, and I grimaced
till I smiled, grimaced till I laughed
grimaced till I let my father
pull me to him, crying into his shirt.
I could only say *Dad, dad.*
I meant love. I was sick with it.

■

The curled birch bark fascinated
the boy in the woods—a piece of wood
he could write on like paper,
write in a wobbly script newly learned,
write the name he could rub his fingers over,
a gift from his father, his alone.

MY MOTHER'S SEE-THROUGH BLOUSE

A rare night out, my older brother
babysitting the rest of us.
My mother emerged from their bedroom
in a see-through blouse,
her plain white bra
clearly visible.

What was she thinking? To wake up
my father's numb shuffle, I guess.

What was she thinking?
My father looked up, jumped,
spilled his coffee.
I was thirteen and couldn't look.

She flushed then paled
trying to keep
from crumbling.

My father didn't yell—
he paced and shook his head
he opened his mouth
he closed his eyes
he made fists.

He sent us to our rooms.
What were you thinking?
he asked her.

I can pile up the facts:
My father was never home.
They were both forty.
She cried. They went nowhere.
We never saw the blouse again.
It was rose-colored.

My mother had one of her
dizzy spells—she lay in bed
all weekend.

My father made us pancakes
the next morning, and they
weren't bad.

He didn't say much.
Kept looking at his watch.
Your mother's sick, he said,
and we knew.

Through the cracked door
I saw him sitting on the edge
of their bed. I couldn't see
her. Nobody said a thing.

Something might have happened
but the next day, it was back
to work, and overtime.

Someone had to cook and clean,
and it was my mother.

Who loved her?
We all did. I lay sleepless
that night, wanting her
normal. I didn't want
to see through.

*Your mother gave us
a scare,* my father said.
I nodded and ate my pancakes,
guzzling my milk
to get the dry pieces down.

POLISH AMERICAN NIGHT, TIGER STADIUM

You and I sit with our girlfriends
in general admission, feeling like old guys
taking our wives to the ballgame—drinking beer,
eating kielbasa, talking about the future.
Twenty years old—me, Debbie, you, Linda,
the summer John Hiller hurt his knee
after striking out five in a row,
the summer you found out Linda liked the Carpenters
not the Kinks and wanted to become a CPA, so
you couldn't possibly get married
because you were obsessed with James Joyce and leaving town,
and Debbie was about to come on to you one drunken night
then deny it later only to end up marrying Mike Dumbowski,
who despite being Polish was not here on Polish American Night
and despite being my good friend
did not resist the advances of hot little Debbie.

No, we do not know all this, just as John Hiller
does not know he'll have a heart attack, but recover
to pitch well enough to become the Tigers' first star reliever,
even though tonight he injures his knee
and goes out for the season.

The crowd is subdued after that.
The kielbasa's greasy and the wind cold.
Debbie and Linda want to leave early,
so we do, without putting up a fight.
And it had started out so good, feeling a little like
old guys taking our wives to the game.

Every time you pitch there's a certain risk involved.
Years later, you look back and can't figure it out.
Like what happened to our friendship.
But I'm glad you wrote me after so many years
to find we still have much in common,
that we both have wives who never liked the Carpenters

and can be counted on not to come on to our friends.
Who could have known Karen Carpenter
was starving herself to death with all that sugary love?
Maybe that's what we were beginning to learn
that night, that loss can come on suddenly
just by bending your leg the wrong way.

SIN SANDWICH

I was in love with my girlfriend's
sister, she rode her bike to the park
to meet me, she didn't have snow tires
we skidded on the picnic table
she was fifteen I was seventeen
I was losing track of my pencils
breaking the leads in my back pocket
her boyfriend had perfect hair
and he knew it
her sister   my girlfriend   well
we were in a glum phase
our eyes tuned to the same TV stories
our friends all coupled up
we squirmed under the pressure
to be happy   to powder our noses and buck up
to not fuck up   well
to be good soldiers   fight the good fight
at least through the prom
at least until the ink dried
on the moustache on the picture
of everyone who said it wouldn't last
she was too straight
I was too crooked
she was too curly   too bouncy
I was too Moe   too Larry
we broke each other's hearts
well   we tried but it was like breaking
a tomato   we smushed each other's hearts
we hurled them at moving targets
through spring and into the dull summer
between lives.

They were both beautiful
I loved them both   I had plenty to go
go around then   the enthusiasm the stamina
the station wagon   but the sister
felt bad and I felt bad
finally we knew there'd be no
smooth transition no ceremony no abdication
no retirement no floats or parades
no conciliatory press conference

she started seeing
a fat guy with good dope during the time
a fat guy with good dope was Mr. Big Stuff
and I was thin and   well   I was skinny
and had average dope   I was an average dope

the thing with the fat guy
had Mr. Hair scratching himself
like a good ballplayer   even seeking me out
for advice   all I could offer was average dope
which he turned down   he married a cheerleader
pregnant   it didn't last long
if only they could have had
perfect hair together first
                              the sister
I could have loved longer
even if she couldn't spell
or because she couldn't
but had the street smarts   street moves
sweet smarts   sweet moves
her sister didn't have
together we blurred all the edges we knew
I loved the guilt   part of me
ate it up   a meal   I could finally digest
that Catholic bug out of my system.

Years later I dreamt the sister
told me she still loved me
I wrote her   spelled out the dream
not mentioning her sister   the girlfriend
she wrote back saying she was secretary
of her church bowling league and was marrying
Mr. Perfect Hair   I'm not lying
and I wrote back   I can't believe I did this
that it was romantic   her getting back
with her old boyfriend after all the years

her sister   the girlfriend   dumped me
for some pretty boy who looked like my older brother
go figure   well also he was a friend of mine
also they ended up married   also they'd been screwing
behind my back   but I had a big back in those days
oh it's always coming and going
going and coming   he was on crutches when I found out
so I couldn't even kick his ass and who knows
he might've been able to beat the shit out of me
with one of those crutches   I'm no tough guy
and after all who's calling the kettle names
or however that goes
                    the last time I wrote her
was to congratulate her on her marriage
hey no hard feelings
hey, hey, no hard feelings   though
I still get hard feelings thinking of her sister
wearing Mr. Hair's football shirt in the living room
of their house while I sat on the couch with my girlfriend
and watched zombie TV   my girlfriend finally made her
put a robe on   just this long t-shirt
over those perfect legs
                    hey   come on
I'm a human bean   jumping bean
hey you   secretary of your bowling league!

I know I know I'm all talk   like the weathermen
who like to predict snowstorms   who like to gloat
over record highs and lows   they love natural disasters
my life has been a natural disaster nyuk nyuk nyuk
I have lusted in my heart and outside my heart
I have not stepped behind the purple confessional curtain
to lay out my sins in years   let me keep
my sins the first day of spring and it's snowing
I'll take the sister over the girlfriend any time
again I'll take the stupid crazy lust any time
give me that old-time religion give me those old-time
hard feelings the religion of two bodies the religion
of the three stooges   the three of us troubled by love
and blood and desire for blood and desire
for the Curly shuffle the Curly scuffle
on the floor   in the back seat
in the park our jeans   grass-stained
our butts wet with dew   there's no shocking the moon
I know but I think we surprised him mildly once or twice
oh lord lust has got to be okay or I'm in big trouble
oh lord give me a rug-burn sandwich
give me a wet tongue sandwich   I'm thirsty
for saliva and sweat straight up   just give me a dark closet
and let me be creative   buried under a pile of coats
give me a quick hip shake   a bump-and-grind burger
lock me up   put me out of my misery
just slide a sin sandwich under the door
just enough sin to live on.

HOW

he proposed to her at a train crossing
as she sat behind him on his Harley
but she didn't hear him above the train's
roar and he bumped his helmet against hers
when he turned to repeat the question
shouting it, indisputable after months of hedging
and how he turned forward again
waiting till she said yes and how
he wanted to kiss her but the train was gone
so he revved up and crossed the bumpy tracks

and how his wife was leaving him now after
15 years and how he'd messed up bad
a few years back with another woman and how she kept
throwing that in his face again now suddenly
because this time it was her
her in love with someone else
tooth for tooth stick in the eye
and how driving the truck lately
he wanted to not slow down
on some exit ramp, keep barreling on
till he was dead and this was over

and how his older boy suspected something
and what could he ever say to him,
his family crumbling into pebbles, then fine dust
and how he couldn't breathe without choking
and how they were the only couple
still married among their high school friends
and how shocked everyone would be and how he gave her
diamond earrings for their anniversary last month
and how she cried knowing it was no use
and how on the road in the truck he imagined her
with the other faceless man and how, strangely,
he could sleep now, the insomnia gone
how sleep was his escape and how he daydreamed

about the peace of sleep, about how he wished
he'd never given up the guitar
and how he'd been safety boy of the year
when he was 10 years old and how that's
the last time he got an award for anything
and how he knew he was feeling sorry
for himself but couldn't help it

and how he'd given up all drugs
even pot because he wanted something
to be clear and how he'd stayed with his wife
broken off his affair, a final choice
and how relieved he was not to have the guilt
scraping at his insides but how she'd brought
the guilt back now and it still worked
how it still dug and bulldozed

and how he wished he'd tried college
15 years ago instead of marrying,
but how he still loved his wife no matter,
and how he'd always loved driving, her hands
on his waist on the back of the bike
and how he'd cured his restless heart
but now she'd caught it and it wasn't going away
and how riding his Harley it just seemed light
and empty, the breeze stinging his face
the helmet too tight

and how he loved his kids
and took them fishing though one got seasick
and how he cradled the sick one's damp head
as he bent over the side of the boat
gentle and how he wanted someone to cradle his head
just like that and how he wished he could vomit up
all the badness and be done with it
and how he was disappointing his parents
one more time and how he was looking for a new job
because business was bad and how he was 40 years old
and the skin on his face was tightening

into creases and how his beard was sprinkled with gray
and how tired he was and just wanted to sleep
but he had at least four more hours of driving
and how he picked up his CB and pressed the microphone
and said *Hey, hey, anybody out there?*

NIGHT LIGHT

-for Mrs. Nesta

Up late again, I sit on the toilet
flicking your night-light
on and off in the little pink bathroom
under the stairs. I am writing
on the little scraps of paper
you left by the phone.
We do not use the night-lights
you left to dot these halls.

We are taking care
of your old house. Last week
we bought a bedroom set off an old widow
moving in with her brother. Cherry wood.
Maybe you know her? Mrs. Santoro.
A scapular hung over the bedpost—
it must have been her husband's.
I gently lifted it, draped it
over a stack of boxes.

I wanted to put that scapular on.
Can you understand that? I wanted
to drape it over my neck
and say a few prayers for him,
for you, for old people everywhere
selling off their goods.

Are you done with the treatments,
has your hair grown back in?
Will it ever? I worship everywhere.
In the kitchen I pray to the vase you left,
the ceramic woman's head. Her earrings
have dropped off. I have made her
a pair of sunglasses and taped them on
so she will not see us scuff your floors.

Sometimes we still come across a note
you left us—instructions for the stove,
the furnace, the floodlights, the locks.
I heard how the gypsies robbed you
when you let them use your phone.
But that's not why you sold this
for a prayer.

The absence of your grandfather clock
ticks in the hallway. You called to ask
for the catalogs you use to shop.
We'd thrown them out. We are young
and small in this big house,
but we will fill it up with our dust and sins.

In this tiny room under the stairs
I flick off the light and step out
into the dark hall, feeling my way.
It is time again to dump the bag of keys
you left, to finger your old bones.

COMING HOME FROM THE HOSPITAL AFTER MY SON'S BIRTH

The chimney next door tilts
precarious, just
like it did yesterday.

In the street, a red sports-
car revs and stalls,
good for a laugh.

I wipe my tears.
I strum a very tiny
air guitar.

SILK

No relative of mine, my wife's father's
cousin's wife.

The silk blouse we brought you from America
sent you into an ecstasy
of vanity, trying it on, twirling
in front of us, your puffy face
crinkling with joy. You made us
take your picture over and over
while your husband lay sick in his robe
gray on the bed, leaning against a torn pillow.

You seemed obsessed with dollars
and America: *How much for this?*
For this? You'd make a great Republican,
I thought, as you prattled about royal blood
somewhere back in time.

You told your husband
I will wear this to your funeral.
We blanched. *I will be beautiful*
at your funeral, you said.
We left you both in the almost-silence
of rustling silk, rustling sheets.

Six months later, dead. You,
not him. Did they bury you in that blouse,
all dressed up, cancer feasting inside you?

Who am I to judge, having grown up
free and full? Silk, *svila,*
you kept repeating, a chant, a spell
to take you out of the tiny apartment
where you'd raised the only child
you could afford, *svila,* dancing
through the two rooms of your life.

America is not Dallas,
I shouted above the blaring TV.

Why is it I expect the poor
not to be selfish?
I'm sorry for the face I made.

Maybe you wanted to make him mad enough
to stay alive. Thank you
for the cream puffs—they were good.

THE SLEEPER HOLD

Every night in Italy, we watched
Colpo Grosso, a striptease game show.

No heat in that old stone house
except a drafty fireplace
and a tiny wood stove. We curled
up for warmth in our long silk underwear.
Seeing them dance naked
on the screen, we imagined
the warm thrill.

On *Big-Time Wrestling,* The Student,
a masked wrestler, applied the Sleeper hold
to end his matches. Subtle, almost intimate,
after body slams and flying dropkicks.
He wrapped his arms around the neck and shoulders
and gently squeezed his victim off to sleep.

What a way to earn money for college.

I imagined us as caterpillars
weaving our silk cocoon, readying
for a deep sleep. The scorpions
tucked themselves into our shoes,
under plants, the dark moist spots.
Scorpions can live a year without food.
I wore a hat to cover my ears.
The whispered hiss of fire,
the soft collapse of wood into gray ash
your breath, and soft,
your breath, and sleep.

■

I worked in an auto factory
to pay my way through college.
At work, they called me
The Student.

I did not wear a mask.
I wore earplugs and gloves
and steel-toed boots
like everyone else.

We took pills
to keep us awake, gobbled them
like lab mice at the feeder.
We called them vitamins.

How did I end up in Italy?
I was searching for dark,
moist places. I was tired of calling things
by the same old names.

■

Bobo Brazil, his pomaded hair
slicked back, was the only black wrestler
then. They treated him as an exotic.
His special move was the Coco Butt.
He butted The Student into submission.

Bobo was a good guy, a true gentleman.
He picked up my friend Rex hitchhiking once.
Rex said he was a gentle man
in person. What a difference
a space makes.

Anyone with a mask was a bad guy.
They booed The Student:
Oh no! The Sleeper hold!

I have never slept better
than under that huge pile of blankets
in that stone house in Italy.

My wife is beautiful
in long blue silk.
We match. We swim toward
the blue lagoon.

We are contenders
for each other's love.

The Student didn't stick around long.
I suppose he graduated
and works as a chiropractor.

Once you're in the Sleeper
you never get out.
Wrestling is not fake.

Let me say it again—
wrestling is not fake.
Think about it.

It's as real as life insurance.

To wake his victim, The Student
draped a black cloth over the head
and did some manipulations
till the sleeper shook his head, groggily
stumbled out of the ring.

■

I didn't stick around long
in the factory. I stumbled out
every night after work, asleep still,
asleep already.

The silence in Italy,
the opposite of what I heard there.
The stones in that old house
haven't moved in 500 years.

■

Umberto Smaila hosted
Colpo Grosso with an admirable
sleaze, his black moustache
the tail of a scorpion.

Impatient for more skin,
we booed when he sang his nightly song.
He crooned on, oblivious.

We rooted for our favorites,
color nearly rising in our cheeks.
We loved the flesh we saw,
we loved the flesh we didn't see.

■

We were rarely naked
those winter months, our skin
grew like white asparagus,
exotic, rare, hidden from light.

The television was our crystal ball
to someplace warm. We polished
the screen with imagined sweat.

■■

Every morning, the black cloth
of our sleep is lifted. Every day
that same miracle.

The woman I love
sleeps beside me.
I curl around her.
Moist, dark. We hold
each other. We warm
each other. Wrestling
is real. The soft whispers
of our fire.

Blink once, blink twice,
and we're gone.

7

BLUE JESUS

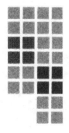

YELLOW JESUS

Can you keep a secret?
I have seen halos around the heads
of beautiful women. Okay, shoot me
with a well-intentioned folk song—
I'm telling the truth
till it hurts: I love the body.
I love the sonic boom boom
of the heart after skin touches skin.

::

When I was young and my pores
clogged with pure impurity,
I took pleasure in squeezing out
the pus, though you're not supposed
to squeeze. We all know
the poison's in there. It was nice
to see some of it come out
now and then, and wipe it away,
and imagine I might live
thirty more good seconds.

::

We have stained the walls of churches
with candle smoke for a long time
and counting. A little bit of hell
to heat up the holy water. I try to keep
the faith *and* keep the fires burning.

::

Yellow Jesus,
is the sun Your good eye,
and the moon Your evil eye?
Some mornings I stand naked at the window

while my favorite saint sleeps on,
and I see them both in the clear blue,
my two yellow friends,
and I could believe in anything.

GREEN JESUS

has been erased from the hymnals
and turned into a three-prong outlet.
The lustful priest hid Him in his guitar
at the folk mass, but no one was fooled.
His sweat nourished the rectory's house plant
while they broke him down and he confessed.
Back to the organ's stomp and shriek.
Green Jesus guzzles poison, then reappears
between sidewalk cracks. Green Jesus
of the hillside and meadow, the smooth curve,
the beautiful chaos. He accepts no folded letters.
He says *why not admit your ignorance?*
He whispers *this is as loud as it gets*. The lustful
priest happily goes deaf. Green Jesus stains the knees
of the blessed children. When you call Him,
He does not answer. He is sarcasm's greatest enemy.
He is the circular prayer, the spinning wheel.
We make our money green. We call green lucky.
We call it inexperienced. We scrub it out.

PURPLE JESUS

Jesus, I'm not done with you.
Are you done with me?
Last week I stopped in a church
to look at a box they say
holds some holy bones
just to say I was there.

You have to take it on faith
that I was there, that I saw the box,
that the bones were in the box,
that the bones were St. Valentine's,
that St. Valentine was a holy man,
holy enough to join the frat,
that the people who let him in
weren't fools to begin with,
filling each other's underwear
with shaving cream.
You see what I'm saying?
I haven't even got anywhere near
what it takes to believe in You.

▓

I walked in to the smell
of Purple Jesus
rising in sweet incense
like one beautiful letter
repeating itself above our heads.
Purple Jesus makes me shut up
and admire the dust I'm headed for.

My mother can't kneel anymore.
She sits during the kneeling parts—
on the edge of the pew so she's not quite
comfortable, so her knees almost
touch the kneeler. She believes

the somber Purple Jesus knows
she'd be kneeling
if it didn't hurt
quite so much.

██

Purple Jesus, my favorite crayon.
You don't make me a soldier
in your army. You don't ask for
the numb repeated prayer.
You simply want my sadness.

I go in churches as a tourist
to look at art made in Your name.
One Good Friday I stood in back
with my arms crossed, and an angry
man made me unfold them.
If that's all it takes
to dis You,
I'm in trouble.

██

We don't get to see the Purple Jesus
very often, though when I smoked
a lot of pot, I imagined I saw Him often.

I meant no disrespect.
I mean no disrespect.
Lord have Mercy.
Christ have Mercy.

If I was going to rise from the dead,
spring would be the time.
I am writing a name in the layered sunset.
Mine, not His.

WHITE JESUS

is only visible to the naked eye.
Smells like bleach and soap
and sperm, the clean ironed cloth
of ceremony.

White Jesus is a theory. The fifth base.
The finger pointing into space.
The wall of unspoken apology.
The shirt worn to funerals.

My young children wrapped in towels
after a bath, waiting to be lifted up.
A white sheet blown horizontal,
clothespins holding tight

against the myth of rising up
if only they'd let go.

SHEDDING THE VESTMENTS

I was inside her for the first time
when her parents pulled up the driveway.

Her father's brain was the size of a small stone
dug up by an idiot pig. He greeted me cordially.

For those brief seconds I felt the warmth
I would lie and betray and nod and wink

and shuffle and grin and make cheat sheets for,
juggle chainsaws on my unicycle for.

Some of us have a talent for being naked.
Others have a talent for imagining nakedness.

There was nothing gentle about what we did,
frantic explosions under the flashlights of policemen.

Didn't they have something better to do?
When would there ever be anything better to do?

I had a talent for getting lost and making jokes
along the way. Anyone who's going to hell,

follow me, I used to say. The teachers ripped
my test papers from my hands. I never had

enough time. After that, her mother wouldn't
let me in the house. I stood on the curb

talking to her while her father cut the grass
as short as his hair. We never got that close

again. A stupid boy got her pregnant,
and it wasn't me. I looked at my watch

and sighed. I signed my name to an agreement
to obey traffic signs and crossed myself

as if I believed in something other than
that warmth, that dark wet heaven

that shrunk my brain to the size of a pebble
even that pig would know better than to dig up.

It was me alone in my bed banging my head
against the gates. I am sorry if I disturbed

you, you with something better to do.
You who own the moon's flashlight

and the hammer of dawn. Listen, hear
the zippers falling, the air hissing

out of the slow leak of what we were told
about goodness. Or maybe it's just somebody

alone, remembering and sighing.
Everyone who's following me,

go to hell.

NIGHT JANITOR, MCMAHON OIL

No one working late tonight. I mean,
except us, but some say we don't work here,
we just clean. Air freshener stinks up

the tiny men's room where lawyers miss, piss
on the floor. I make the steel shine. Jack vacuums
spot theory—he's done in minutes.

I know a few faces here, late-nighters
with their tired smiles. What are they
doing to celebrate this spring evening?

We're going fishing. I steal a roll of toilet paper
for home. Gravel crunches under us in the empty lot.
We spin out. For the hell of it.

Along the banks of the Pine, near Tipton Bridge,
no bass or pike tonight. We catch bluegills,
throw them back.

The company brought in Red Adair once,
the famous oil-fire fighter. Everyone wore hard hats
for pictures with Red to hang on office walls.

There are no pictures with guys holding cleanser
posed around a toilet, but I'd like to see one of those.
I'd like to see one of those guys piss straight.

■

Jack lost his CETA job working with deaf workers
because there is no CETA anymore. He's taught me
a few signs. *I love this,* he signs. It's nice

that he doesn't have to speak.
Jack gets letters about his loans. They burn like any paper.
I rest my head in my hands and smell cleanser.

Friends passed this job on to us, a couple
who got better jobs and moved on. This job
not enough to live on. We both work days,

minimum wage. *Every three months
you can steal one can of coffee,* our friends said.
We will leave this job as soon as something

comes up. That's a wish. Something
to come up. Tonight I wish my hands smelled
like the river. I let them drag in cold water

but it's not enough. If I catch enough fish
and let them go, my hands will smell like fish.
That's the deal I make tonight. Or maybe just my wish.

▓

The fish slide out of my hand and flop back
into the dark river. If I am a fish, I am a bluegill.
If you've ever fished, you've caught a bluegill.

And if it was your first fish, maybe someone let you
keep it, if it was big enough. Most likely
you threw it back. If it didn't swallow the hook.

It's my goal never to swallow the hook.
Jack has to leave soon because he's in love.
She has long blonde hair, and paints black canvases,

tends bar at the Pine Knot
and slides us a pitcher or two.
I would like to be in love tonight

but I will settle for my hands smelling like hands.
I will settle for a new roll of toilet paper,
the soft kind, my bonus to myself.

Instead of a cleaning service,
they settled for us. We work cheap, settle
too easily. The office keys rattle in my pocket.

They're alright, the ones I've met,
sweating over figures. Tonight I want
to be generous like the river and let things be.

Before we get in the car, we stand for a moment,
water rushing past below us.
My hands smell a little like fish, a little like cleanser.

I cup them against my face while Jack drives.
You praying again? he says.
It's a joke—he's never seen me pray.

Yeah, I say. I want to make a joke,
but I just say *yeah.*

THE FALL

Tonight I look down
from the upstairs window
at the snow angel
I fell to make in the yard
now lit by moonlight,
glistening.

What glorious wings.
What a tiny fucking head.

BONE AND HOOK

(Triptych, 1981)

1

Blood trails from beneath the door
like the spray paint of Jesus Christ.

Like an unlit fuse. Like the seventh veil.
And the door is open.

What anyone could see is black
but some of us imagine light

further back.

2

If my ears had hands, what
would they reach for?
If my knee had a pocket, what
would I store there?

If my toes were tiny flashlights,
I'd still have to crouch to see.

Blood forms a red sheet,
a banner for the worst causes.

I am the poster child
for the willfully deformed
I am the line not to be crossed
I have signed away all rights
I have absolved everyone
of liability.

My spine has been surgically removed.

I've got a box of bodily fluids
ready to mail to the underworld.

A few more orifices couldn't hurt.

3

My goal is human jello.
The heart my favorite mold.

A foot stretched into taffy.
The handiness of a hook
randomly placed.

Randomness is handy.
I've replaced my spine
with a door jamb.

That window is really
a yield sign.

I've hooked a big one.

The door opens to pure black,
the window to pure light.

I'm standing in the foyer
of the blues, spitting out
my gum and ready to jump.

My toes are melting,
and I ain't goin' nowhere.

Jesus Christ—He tossed
my bones in the darkness
and said *fetch*.

THE BLACK HOLE OF THE HUMAN BODY

(Head II, 1949)

it bore into the leg cast
of a little girl who didn't look
both ways

it was displayed
on the ribs of a bullfighter
and in the open mouths
of the stunned crowd

it appeared as an oil stain
on a gas station calendar
obscuring another
manufactured holiday

the puckered anus
of a bored junkie posing
in a porn magazine

the cancerous lesion
on the cheek
of a self-portrait

the scar of dried snot
pulled from the nose
of the filthy man
with two clean dogs
washing himself
in the playground fountain

it's not going away
so we may as well
plunge our wrists in it

we may as well wave to the shadow
loitering under the streetlight
and call it in.

EVOLUTION: TWO FIGURES WITH MONKEY

(Two figures with a monkey, 1973)

Every lightbulb is a hammer
pounding in the regret

of the smudged chalkboard
of last night's blurry

binge that put you here
unclothed and stunned

like that tired wasp
buzzing slow against the window.

The water tap seems impossibly far away.
Our forced smiles crackle at each other.

The tinfoil of our brains
tries to unball itself.

Wouldn't it be great if we were
in love? Wouldn't it be great

if that spring wasn't poking through
the mattress? Has anyone ever told you

your hair looks like a dead pheasant?
I didn't know you smoked dynamite.

A monkey walks up the stairs with the mail,
his smile more like a squint, his chattering

more like speech. He carries letters
saying *no* and *give*. He waits

by the side of the bed—got a buck
for the kid? I ask. Can you do anything

about that blue hole in the wall?
you ask. They call that a window, I say.

The monkey vanishes. All that's left
is his tail, a stick floating in blue water.

My head on your quiet chest,
my ear warming. Simultaneous breathing.

Then, wind in the open door
calling us names, everything we deserve.

JET OF WATER

(*Jet of water,* 1979)

I am in love
with any fountain
I am promiscuous
with fountains
I have made my wish
I have tossed my coin
I have witnessed the small
splash and gentle sinking

I am in love
with the simplicity
of fountains
water into air
a dribble or a shot
release relief repeat
the mist of vague dreams

let me take you there
(let me take you there)
lit by evening and fragile sin
(lit by the one forgiving eye)
and if we wade in the pool
(and if we wade in the pool)
will we receive a saving grace
(will we give a saving grace)

oh Lord when I die
(when I die)
leave the water running

8

NIGHT WITH DRIVE-BY SHOOTING STARS

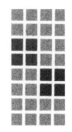

RED VINYL

–for Peter Wolf

Ain't nothing but a party
ain't nothing but a party
ain't nothing but a house party.

We danced in aisles, on seats, shouted
ourselves raw. The next day, ears ringing,
we sat stunned in dull classrooms,
listening to the drone of old English poets
telling us some shit about love.
Our teacher talked about the iamb
when we wanted the *I am*
you sang about while Magic Dick moaned
on his harp, his afro a breaking wave
as he rocked, as he blew and blew.

That ringing in my ears was poetry
I know now–pissed off and boasting–
poetry with shades on. You danced
crazy over the stage–them's the feet
I thought were neat–you spouted
you shouted rhythm and blues rhymes.

We were stupid white boys who worked on cars
and had no imagination, who did poorly in school
without even style to fall back on.
We packed monster stereos into our junker cars
and rocked loud enough to sing along without shame
while in English class we whispered and stuttered.

Your best album, *Bloodshot,* stamped
on red vinyl, circled our turntables
in damp basements like a neon cherry–
our futures, plain black vinyl, already
a little warped, bald tires and bad news,
dirty oil and rust. Why not shout a little first,
telling wild stories at parties where I could

lose the point, get a laugh, a laugh
and maybe a red kiss from a mixed-up girl
with dirty blond hair—she's kissing everyone
but I don't care. I take it home, my ears ringing.
I write that kiss down, pressing hard.

QUITTING THE CARD CLUB

My brother and I fetched
the neighbors' card tables, squeezed
four of them into our front room.
My mother put out ashtrays
and Spanish peanuts, fretting over
the tight squeeze, scolding when we shed
the red skins over the clean floor.
Later, we lay in bed, smoke
and laughter snaking under
our closed door, metal chairs screeching
against the wood.

Mrs. Bruno told a story she thought
was funny: My brother and I had asked
if she wanted us to shovel her snow.
She said *how much?* We said
whatever you think is fair
and shoveled her walk and driveway.
She gave us fifteen cents.

We stared into our numb hands
and walked away, sweat freezing
under our collars. We'd told no one.

■

Do you think that was fair?
my mother asked. *Do you think
that was fair to two little boys?*

They should have known better,
Mrs. Bruno said.
*Should have known better
than to trust a bitch like you,*
my mother said.

■

The next day, we hauled those tables back.
The neighbors did not offer us cookies,
sent home no message of thanks.
We felt like we did squeezing
that dime and that nickel.

You might think my mother would've slipped us
something then, but she never gave us money.
It was that way in our family.
My father was home early for a change—
he and my mother in the kitchen,
smoking, drinking. She was laughing.
Good for you, my father said.
She was crying. *Good for you,* he said.

HEAT WAVE

Martha Reeves and the Vandellas
sang *Nowhere to run, nowhere*
to hide while riding in a convertible
gliding down an assembly line
at a factory in Detroit. I didn't begrudge them
their sparkly dresses—they were just singing
the truth and making some bucks to boot.
I study the guys on the line around them
in the video clip. They must have been instructed
not to look. To do their jobs.
                          I must be out
of camera range. I sang loud but no one
gave a shit. I sang "Heatwave" I sang "Quicksand."
I bowed to the power presses and accepted
how they shook the earth. An ordinary man,
I worried the hands on my clock till they grew
thin and brittle. My gloves smudged the world black.
The drugs I took dressed the world in sequins.

HELPING WITH MY BROTHER'S RÉSUMÉ

Truck driver, I typed,
and the years.

Perfect driving record.
Loaded and unloaded trailer.
Assisted on supply orders.

(pause)

Drivers' Safety certificate course.
Evaluation of equipment.
Log-book regulations.
Scheduling.

()
()

Collecting cans for the Salvation Army.

()
()
()

Graduate, Fitzgerald High School.

()
()
()
()

His two boys? Work with the scouts?
Little league coaching?

He shrugs, I shrug. He sweats,
I sweat, to fill one page:
a little boldface, a little italics.
Bump up the font size. Extra white space.

We print it up, and he grins
at its professional look. He points
and his finger smudges the page.

He blushes. A life.
We print it up again—
clean, perfect.

BEAUTIFUL THING

My first child collects snail shells
under a sun the color of the shirt
before the blood, rinsing them
like a priest washing his hands
before the miracle.

He raises each white shell
for me to admire. I wash my face
with his soft skin. The wetness
and the glow.

He is a pure guitar string
echoing in the shell of the hollow body
where someone lived once,
then left this beautiful thing.
Imagine the sound.

FALLING BRICKS

My daughter sings under the brick arch
of the abandoned house next door,
her stage for an audience of stones
and weeds. Her voice through glass
high and griefless, higher than it
might ever go, the sky endless
pure blue without credit cards
or betrayal.

Who can you trust? I'm making a list
of things to do—it helps me
keep control. I fold up the list
and toss it in the trash with a piece
of broken glass. When she is tired,
my daughter clutches my neck
as if it were a rope to save her.

The song has more than one name,
if we have to put a name on it,
write it down—three songs
intermingled and strung together
seamlessly, like I imagine our lives
should be, mine, hers, and down
the line.

Above her, the bricks
are loosening. I should not
let her sing there, but she is perfectly
framed, like a saint in an altar.
I hold my own neck like that
to imagine the comfort she takes.
My skin is loosening there.
Oh, my beautiful child,
do not trust me.

BETWEEN PERIODS

Last night, a friend called
to say she's dying of brain cancer.

Someone is drilling through the still
summer air. The sound clenches
my teeth. It's going in cleanly.
Only a small hole.

My daughter pretends to wash
her hands. As if it were that easy
to wash off the dirt of this world.
She's laughing and wants me
to laugh too, to share the joke
like her first secret.

My friend asked if I was watching
the big playoff game
between my team and her team

before she told me she's dying.
I said *no, I'm watching my kids.*
That must have sounded

a little cold. First time her team's
made the finals. My kids were screaming
about who goes first, who's the leader.

She was hysterical over a hockey game,
suddenly a big fan. We've got some crazy birds
here who start chirping early—not even
close to morning, not a glimmer

of light anywhere. *What the hell is she
doing,* I ask my wife, as if she's to blame.
What the hell is she doing

with cancer? She has a teenage son.
They were watching the game
together. Who's drilling what
on this lazy afternoon? What makes

it lazy? If it's lazy, does that make it
slower for the dying? It's my birthday.
My kids are downstairs making me a crown.

The doctors talked her out of chemo.
She can still eat. She's lost a lot of weight.
I look good, she said. I didn't know what

to say on the other end.
Oh Debra, Oh Debra, I said
as if repetition could keep her

here. On this earth. I want to be a spike
nailed to it, but it's my birthday—
I'm a stick man with a stick cane.

My son collects sunshine in baskets,
offers me some. I count the states
between us. Will I see her again?
I put on my crown, tilt it
at a jaunty angle. We practice

blowing out the candles. I clean off the Z
on my keyboard. It doesn't get used much.
The A looks great. *Hey kids, let's not answer
the phone, hey kids, let's wash our hands
before we eat.*

She knows what's up. She's keeping
her hair, dyeing it blond
like she always wanted. *Fuck 'em,*

she said, and started to cry.
It was between periods.

They were going to start up again soon—
she had to go, go, go.

Hope your team wins, I said,
even if it means beating mine.

Fuck 'em, I agreed, and there was nothing
more to say.

I lay sleepless in twisted sheets.
3:00 A.M. The birds were chirping.
Already? I said.

BROWN'S FARM

I drive past the orchard, then swerve off
the road to circle back. Sunday morning,
everyone in church except us and Mr. Brown.
We are on a drive to nowhere, our two children
strapped in behind us, eyes wide with silence.

The sign says *Open 2–5,* but she tells me
to ask the man behind us mending fences.
We've been fighting over what's wrong with her.
The doctors can't find anything—
asthma? MS? Ulcers? She studies
her hands for signs. They tremble.

What we're left with
spins while we await the latest test results.
Mr. Brown, he doesn't say
We're closed. Can't you read?
He says, *Yes, but we don't have much.*
We must look like people who need
apples. We enter the barn, the dark
fermented smell. He flips on lights
as he leads us to the cooler
where the apples are stored until two.

We shiver. He's talking about apples,
which ones are ready this early
in the season. We buy a peck of Macintosh,
and a jug of frozen cider from last year—
all they have.

We drive off, waving, our smiles
turning real. She passes out apples
and we start crunching. My daughter
is one. I bite the skin off for her.
The car fills with the music of crunching.
Don't choke, we both say.

9

FLAG DAY
IN WARREN,
MICHIGAN:
Uncollected
and New Poems

A REAL COMEDIAN:
THE TRUE GENIUS OF BOB HOPE

(December 1988)

Was he ever really funny? When? I want to know.
Are clowns ever really funny, even to children?
Do you really have to go to college to be a clown?

Why is the president a clown? What training has he had?
Do you really have to go to Hamburger U.?

I had a girlfriend who went on tour with a mime troupe.
For months afterward, she kept making that big O

of surprise. She thought it was cute when I got mad.
O. Let's all be mimes. Or do we have to go

to the Marcel Marceau School of Mimery? The president
is a mime. Look how he holds his hand to his ear

look how he shrugs. Can you guess? He is being
an idiot. Here's the scary part:

that Bob Hope's friend can be president.
That the president can laugh at Bob Hope

like the French laugh at Jerry Lewis.
At least Dean stopped pretending he liked Jerry

at least Bing sang "Drummer Boy" with David Bowie.
Is there a college for becoming Bob Hope?

Is his vault full of jokes there, a whole vault
without one chuckle? Bob entertained the troops

yes, he gets a little good will for that.
They laughed at his jokes, but they were desperate.

How many of them would have showed up
if he didn't have his bimbos along? Bob

always has bimbos. Brooke is his latest.
Look how she shakes her head when she smiles.
It's called acting.

The president married a ghost and hosted
Death Valley Days. 20 Mule Team Borax—
What does that mean? I have never understood

the true genius of his acting ability.
I have never understood why America voted for him

twice. Who's pulling his strings? His head
shakes suspiciously like Brooke's.

All the bimbos on his specials know how to make the O.
Bob tells a joke, they make the O.

O Bob you are old and I should not make fun of you
but you are still on TV. What's so special
about your specials? Maybe you were good in the '40s

or '50s, or even the early '60s. Maybe you were funny
then, before Vietnam. Packy East. I like that name.

A real name. A lousy boxer. A bad mime. The whole country's
falling apart, and we're stuck with you and George Burns.

We're stuck with you and George Bush. We're stuck
with Bush and Dan Quayle. Dan and Brooke.

Bob, you won't go away. You won't take your millions
and millions and leave us alone. You are so rich

it makes me so sad. You have to be rich
to be the president's friend, the president for 8 years—

count 'em. 1. 2. 3. 4. 5. 6. 7. 8—has made me so sad
I am losing my words, I am losing

my O of surprise. All I can do
is the scene where the walls are closing in.

THE TENURED GUY

I have smiled
and said hello in the hallways
I have lost sleep over brief exchanges
I have changed pants
just to pick up my mail
and I have gotten tenure.

I have kept my one good pair of shoes
and my corduroy sport coat in my office
just in case. I have nodded
at the names of authors
I have not and will never read
and I have gotten tenure.

I have kept my nose clean,
literally. I have sipped wine
at department parties and receptions
staying just long enough.
I have sat in the back at lectures
far enough away to really not hear
and I have nodded astutely.
I have never asked a question
or disagreed with anyone
in any of the long
Meetings of the Living Dead
and I have gotten tenure.

I have served on committees
with a smile, oh, always
with a smile. I have blended
into the beige paint
I have become the beige paint
subtly, so subtly
I'm not sure where
the paint stops and I begin.

I have gotten tenure
and it's my own fault.

Even as I write this
I am not sure anyone will ever see it.
But why should I care
now that I have gotten tenure?
I am so used to caring
I don't know if I can stop.

I have rounded off my grades upward
to avoid the student complaint
and I have gotten tenure.
I have been a nice guy in class
to students majoring in whining
and I have gotten tenure.

I have published bad work
and I have gotten tenure.
I have padded my vitae—
what I used to call my résumé—
and I have gotten tenure.

My friend Tom quit teaching
and became a waiter
only to get his jaw busted after work
by an unknown assailant. He once said
the ideal job would be to teach half the time
and haul garbage the other half.
He's teaching again now.

I have kept secrets, I have covered up
I have been bored to death
I have been attacked by unknown assailants
behind my back, I have started to grit my teeth
grind my teeth I am wearing them down
the fangs are dulling
but I have tenure.

Half my friends hate me for getting tenure.
They think I'm lucky or that I sold out.
Maybe they're just jealous or maybe
I'm just paranoid. I would like workman's comp
for paranoia. I have been injured on the job
I have been injured on the way to tenure
I have gotten lost on the way to tenure
I am still waiting for the official letter
I am still waiting for the map
I am still waiting to find my way home.

I have cut back on my *ain'ts* and *yeahs*
I have discussed my work in an intellectual fashion
I have talked about my place in American literature
I have talked about breaking new ground
I have ranked myself very highly
the dean said *top ten* so I said *top ten*.

I once said all I wanted to do was teach and write.
A Full Professor laughed at that.
How naive, I'm sure she was thinking.
Maybe someday I'll be a Full Guy
and I'll be able to sit
with the other Full Guys and Full Gals
and have a Full Meeting. Oh I have a hard on
just thinking about it.

I have tenure, did I tell you that?
I explain it to my family and they nod:
You can never be fired, great. Oh,
I am in the club now, my referees
have blown their whistles in my support
I am studying the secret handshakes and codes
I am growing a beard so I can stroke it wisely
while I vote on another person's fate.

When you see me walking down the hall, say
Hey, there's the tenured guy! And I will give you
my little tenured wave, not too exuberant—
just so long, so high.

SKYWRITING

Marrying at 19, he hired a skywriter
    to scrawl I LOVE YOU across
        the hazy factory sky of Warren, Michigan,

then moved into his in-laws' basement.
    Divorced in three years,
        and she kept the cute little dog.

Or maybe a helicopter dropped
    a thousand balloons onto the street
        or he took her away

in a hot-air balloon. Whatever. Warren
    had seen nothing like it.
        His gay brother Arthur

was still in the closet theoretically,
    and his other brother theoretically
        had come out of rehab clean.

Everyone emerged
    from their houses and stared at the sky
        like the second coming

of Devon or Timmy Jay was happening
    up there (twins shot by their
        stepma). We all smiled

and shook our heads, hands on hips
    or raised to the sky like
        can you believe it?

It couldn't have been a hot-air balloon
    with all those telephone wires
        criss-crossing like burnt spaghetti

or Mr. Dunn's bad combover. Everybody—
    I mean everybody—I know how people
        say everybody and just mean like

most of the people—said it wouldn't last.
    Karen squeezing his hand,
        her teeth already a gritty smile—

she wasn't even pregnant, they insisted truthfully.
    But then why start out in a basement?
        Even true love couldn't last

in a basement in Warren, what with
    the floods and all. The mold and spiders,
        the old *Playboy*s stuffed in the rafters,

the swap-meet guns, the plastic weight set
    from Sears, the blood-stained washtubs,
        rusty buckets, crickets, unmatched

sneakers, backwash beer bottles lined in a case,
    ripped ironing board, cracked casement windows,
        cigar boxes stuffed with legal and illegal papers.

It was a helicopter. And roses, I think. Hundreds,
    and how could he afford it? Asshole.
        Okay, goddamn it, I'm the other

brother, I can call him that. I could've blown
    bubbles at them and taken the money
        and got high for the next couple of years.

Everybody knew it wouldn't last,
    but that doesn't mean a few of us
        didn't get choked up.

The skywriting dissipated
    into thin air. Or the balloons
        blew away. The roses hit

with a thud. We backed away from the noise.
   As it lifted back up and flew away
      we helped gather what had fallen.

THE BEGINNINGS OF COMPASSION

Do you feel it for an ant?
A ladybug? A fly? A bee? A cricket?
A grasshopper?

Ladybug. So, it's not just size.
Who's got the prettiest face
on death row?

A squirrel? A rat?
A mouse? A sparrow?
I stop at the rabbit.
I would like to go lower

but I stop at the rabbit.

⚏

Okay, no capital punishment
for creatures with spots
and quiet hoppers. Not for butter-
flies, but yes for moths.

Men over 6 feet 6
with scars? IQs below 32?
For anyone who's fucked with
my family?

⚏

While I was away, a sparrow made a nest
in the awning outside my back door.
Each time I opened the door
it flew in the house,

up the staircase, bouncing
off walls, windows. I trapped it

against the bathroom tile,
released it outside.

Found it dead the next day. Tossed
the nest in the trash like a crown
of thorns constructed by a Jesus-wannabe.

■■

I smashed a snake with a big rock once.
Never shot anything.
Hit small animals with my car.
Maybe a dog once.

Yes, a dog.

God must've given knuckles some thought.
If you believe in him. If you draw the line
somewhere. Are those remnants of the Ark—
or splinters from the True Cross?

A fist. What if it was softer?
Would we knee each other to death?
I idly follow the path of an ant
carrying a crumb across my kitchen floor
before I step on it.

What if our hands could only meet
in a praying gesture, fingers extended,
poking through the air?

We'd all be better divers for one thing.

THE FACTS OF GRIEF

He fired a crabapple into my spokes.
I jumped off my bike and we wrestled
in the driveway, rolled onto the lawn.
My oldest friend.
               His daughter died
last week, blind, a hole in her heart.
14 years of diapers and a carseat.
She was the size of a 3 year old.

When he started punching me,
I grabbed his wrists to protest
but we'd crossed the line.
It wasn't chalk, but a crack in cement.

Carl Mackey was so dumb he thought
we were each other, or at least
brothers.
         Dumb gets redefined,
paper clouds arranged in the sky
to explain the absence of sun.
14 years, he bent to her weak heart
and listened.
             That was my last fight.
His mother came out and broke
it up. I wiped blood on my shirt
and shook his hand.
              We're talking
about that today.
        Not her.
            Not
laughing about it. Our first end
of the world. I'm clutching
the black phone in my fist. *Where
did those crabapples come from?*
he wonders. *We didn't have a tree.*

How long were we mad at each other?
It was a cardboard tree, and the apples
were lollipops. We were stick people
pasted on, our hearts colored
outside the lines,
                             spilling. My blood
was melted popsicles. *The coffin
was so light.*

We knelt together, altar boys
in the dim church, winter mornings.
We believed in everything. What
do I say? I flip clichés like soiled
playing cards, the ends bent and frayed.

No tricks on this end.
                    *Nobody
had a tree,* I tell him. He could listen
all day to things like that,
breathing static on the other end.

THE CHURCH OF MR. PEA

He lives at the center of the universe
twenty miles north of Dayton, Ohio,

or Yuma, Arizona. No one's sure.
He could be living next door.

He's a hard pea. His needs are few.
His father's dead, but he does have

a Holy Spirit—the last tiny breath
of each person dying now/now/now.

Mr. Pea travels eyeball to eyeball.
He never dies himself. Just keeps

getting harder and harder. Still
pretty green, but I wouldn't call it

a miracle. You can worship Mr. Pea
in the privacy of your own home.

Mr. Pea doesn't take up collections.
We all got a little piece of Mr. Pea

inside us. You can decide yourself
how it got there.

Mr. Pea had a feather once.
Any feather could be that feather.

ECONO

I was wandering San Marcos, Texas,
on a Sunday morning. Unshaven
and unshowered, wet with the sudden
storm. A man in a camouflage jacket
trudging toward me across the street—
no sidewalks, just rubble and ditches—
called above the rain. His hair
was my hair, stringy and wild.
His stubble, my stubble. I shook my head
and he called to me again. Should I speed
up? Hurry away? He crossed the street
and I waited. *Do you know if there's
a Salvation Army around here?* he asked.
I said *No, I'm not from here,* and that
was true. I think all the homeless in America
wear camouflage. He thought I was one
like him. I had a hotel room to return to
just around the corner. Hot shower,
and it'd feel good. He was headed
toward town, and I wished him
luck. I have a credit card. More
than one. It's not a very good tool
for digging. You have to have one
to do anything these days.
The Salvation Army. Lord.

I shaved and combed my hair.
I put on dry clothes. I am not from
around here. The rain's pounding
now, bouncing up off cement.
I am staying at an Econo Lodge.
Free coffee and donuts in the morning.
I probably didn't earn that crack
about camouflage. I'd be needing to help
a lot more people to get away with that.
My jacket is blue with a green fleece liner.

I don't know where to go with this
because I did not follow him
down the road.

FLAG DAY IN WARREN, MICHIGAN

Warren—birthplace of white rap star Eminem,
a.k.a. Marshall Mathers, a.k.a. Slim Shady, dropout
of Lincoln High, where even my cousin Earl
made it through

where wind whips an oversized flag
around its pole like a funeral shard
I mean shroud
                and Eminem is arrested twice
for pulling out his unloaded gun and pointing it at
a) a member of the rival group the Insane Clown Posse
b) a man outside a bar who'd been kissing his wife.

on the streets, POW/MIA flags still fly
black and white beneath the r/w/and b.
And the NO SCAB NEWSPAPERS
signs still blot the perfect lawns
five years after the newspaper strike because

we never forget in Warren, goddamn it.
My nephew knows Eminem—has his autograph,
admires him for *telling it like it is*
about gays and women—

rapping lyrics I could be fired for
could be fired for
fired for

*hey perfesser, how you spell
homofobick? missaginest?*

        "This is stuff you might think
        but never say. He's allowed to cross
        that line; he's an entertainer—
        it's his job to cross it."

Let me take you down Mound Road
past the Ford plant, past the Chrysler Plant
where my brother drives large trucks,
past the GM plant, past the newspaper printing plant
where they flew the scab papers out by helicopter
above the screaming protesters, past the Ford axle plant
where my father spent his life, where I spent
enough time to recite Eminem's future lyrics.

MOTHER ON I-94 CHARGED
she killed her baby, police say,

walking naked along I-94
with the dead infant in her arms.

My father's compromise: he does not
subscribe to the paper anymore
but walks to the machine nearly
every day to buy one.

Shards of broken glass mixed
in the playground wood chips
rip open my child's knee,
green space wedged between
two trailer parks on Warner,
which parallels Mound, a mile
and a half away.

10¢ a can recycling, highest
in the country. An old neighbor
pushes a shopping cart full.

"It's offensive to some people—
but not too offensive. It's right
down the middle."

Legalized gambling in Detroit now,
place your bets, throw your money
into the river. Busloads from Warren

pass Detroit to gamble in Canada,
where white people take your money
instead

"The Instead City"
No matter how you dig
there's no mail in that box

grief over an expired coupon
wave goodbye to your kids
disappearing in the distant suburbs
beyond the map's edge

Flag Day in Warren, and tree roots lift sidewalk squares
into crooked patterns like the bad teeth of the real poor
and it's somebody's fault, but who can see beneath
the concrete, into the thick soil where corn once grew
where corn once grew
                              the old farmer's house
still stands. I stood at that door with no bell
and knocked hard, knocked hard and giggled
with school friends as we interviewed the old couple,
the farmer in a wheelchair pissing himself as we talked
and it wasn't so goddamn funny being old
we got the hell out of there as soon as we could
abandoning the kind woman's sour milk
the old man shouting *they plant houses now,*
can you believe it, as we shut the door behind us
and ran, you'd better believe it
and our oral report was a big hit in class.

Aretha the Queen of Soul
has not been paying her bills
at the local merchants',
and the white people say
See?

Number one with a bullet, with a bullet
Eminem an angry punk with a big mouth

and it's all his mother's fault for ditching
him
   bullshit, who ain't been ditched
around here. It's the fucking City of the Ditched
where everybody's a farmer/slave to their lawns,
their unnaturally green squares, neatly trimmed—
don't fall on your knees, you'll be poisoned.

   corrected a judge's pronunciation
   of her daughter's name

My father told the neighbors he was growing
Japanese Dwarf Grass—he never
fertilized or watered. Just let his four boys
pulverize it while he scratched his pencil
into the night, rubbed its bald head
miles away at the plant, the plant, where in the dark
nothing grew.

Eminem and Kid Rock and the Insane Clown Posse,
white rappers from the Detroit *area* making it
on the national scene
                  everybody saying
they're from Detroit when they simply *ain't.*

My nephew's a high school grad unemployed
owner of an eeelectric geetar talkin' 'bout
the community college talkin' 'bout
the CC, the CC, down by the C,
the beautiful C where the grass is somewhat
greener than at the high school.

Twelve Mile High we call it
12 Mile and Schoenner, 3 miles the other side
of Mound. 4 from 8 Mile, the border
with Detroit.

Warren, "The Buy American City"
Warren, "The Gateway to Center Line"

(see, Center Line is surrounded by Warren
so ya gotta drive through Warren to get there
but it looks just like Warren so you're never gonna
know you're there unless you see the tiny sign
welcoming you and kissing your ass goodbye
within the course of four miles.)

Flag Day in Warren and somebody tryin'
sell me somethin' at the door
smilin' and sweatin' but I ain't buyin'

and the mean dog on the corner
locked in the house today—Lord have mercy—
muffled barking. Mean dog not chasin' me
chewin' through the fence.

>   *choked on mud forced down her throat*
>   *and her eyes had been gouged*

Four women in their seventies sitting
on lawn chairs on a cement square porch
survivors of you-name-it
the last white people this close to Detroit
a Tuesday morning in June and they're
grateful it's cool enough and their children
are mostly still alive and their grandchildren
mostly out of jail and nearly employed

and life is good, life is fucking great,
right, Mom? Hey Mom, the phone's for you
Hey Mom, what's for dinner
Hey Mom, can I go out to play
Hey Mom

just kidding, just kidding—she's burning her elbows
in prayer every night for my other nephew
in the juvie home, age 13 and not looking
good, brother. Got the Mark of X on him.

My son takes the stitches. The shroud billows.
No scabs. Roll the dice of blame
and put it to a beat.

POW/MIA

> *neighbors said they couldn't believe . . .*
> *she seemed like a stable . . .*

If I stay here maybe Slim Shady gonna pull
an unloaded gun on me. My father offered me
his old bowling ball, but I turned it down,
Lord, I turned that sucker down. Wanted
to carry it home, sit on it, put my fingers
in the holes, throw a goddamn *strike!*

I live 300 miles away,
but the magnet sucks me back, the famous rap
star sucks me back
           I have spoken
every word he has spoken.

Flag Day in Warren, and the plastic garbage cans
blow in the street, and out front one small boy
spits on another and my sister yells *hey don't*
do that, just don't and the kid looks up
and juices up another gobber and spits it
her way and Robert across the street
taken away by the EMS who drew straws
to see who'd have to go in and get him

(my cousin Earl's EMS now, can you
believe it—got his GED, stopped smoking
all that wacky weed, married someone
who even fucking jogs!)

Hey perfesser, you a fag?

Drunk on the floor in his own shit
among the lounging roaches and empty bottles

and boxes of rags and
                    my father's so happy
they're taking Robert away
he pops open a beer and watches
from the porch, *cheers!*

Flag Day in Warren, and Kevin Neal,
the Slim Shady of the class of '74,
mows his parents' lawn and does not
answer when I call from my car

does not know who I am
and why should he
another ghost in this ghost town

hey perfesser, who your bitch?

things getting blurry
call the cable
get them out here.

Carl Marlinga, county prosecutor,
he's taking it to Eminem
great PR for his State Supreme Court run.

Damn it, Carl, remember me,
I worked in your dad's liquor store
three years. Almost took a bullet
for the old man
                    though the gun
coulda been unloaded
mother fucker
    mother fucker
        gimme the cash

Carl, you remember Kevin?
Kevin, Carl?
We got a variety of erasers here
easy when the lines are so straight
but some of us just erase

forget to write anything new
satisfied with the white slate

Satellite dishes at the trailer park
picking up signals
Eminem tellin' 'em who to blame
no chocolate mess.

    Are you able to see?
    No, I'm not, she responded.

Kevin had the ability to pull unloaded guns
on just about anybody
out of control on the dance floor
now the lawn mower steers him.

chaos, crime on city's land
    makeshift camps, drugs, prostitution
        occupy property

And I am guilty as charged
and I am one of the anointed
with the holy oils of escape
and I help my father repair
cracks in the cement once again

and we have our share of Elvis worship
botched hold-ups and multiple murders
public urination and arson

(if you just take out the punctuation
and confuse the referents
maybe the borders will disintegrate)

    still many unanswered questions

and we have our share of pregnant
teenagers and torn prom dresses
sad shrugs and accidental dismemberment

and today I dive into the dwarf grass
and swim my way through the poison

today I dive into the green carpet
shot by the unloaded gun
murdered by the unloaded gun

Mom on I-94 charged
She killed her baby, police say

and Eminem will get off free
my mean little brother
shooting his way out of here.

SOCK-HOP BLUES

My kids go to private school.
We're financial-aid kids.
I celebrate that to quizzical looks.
I'm quick. I'm Quixote.
They spell fun with a d on the end.
We help out as room parents
to earn our charity. For the sock-hop
I dug out the bowling shirt John Santucci,
my parents' bowling partner, gave me
fifteen years ago. I needed one
for an act I was doing. First time I wore it
since Big John died from asbestos
stabbing his lungs. Slicked my hair back
like Big John, though it probably looked
like more '50s camp. Most of the parents
didn't dress up. The head of the school did.
Efficient poodle skirt. My kids take the bus
to school. When the bus never showed up,
she said it wasn't her problem. It was a fun
raiser for the school. They hired an expensive
DJ. I know because they kept telling me.
Who are they? Am I at least *part*-they?
I bought a car from Big John once.
$300, and he threw in the ice scraper
jumper cables and a gallon of anti-freeze.
I'm sweating like a pig in the gym
though it's not that stuffy. Only kids
dancing, and they're small kids,
pre-deodorant kids. Trickling down
under my arms like it must've when Big John
was throwing strike after strike down
at Bronco Lanes in the mixed-doubles league.
His name in script over my chest. People
are calling me John. It's not so funny
now that he's dead. A guy with black
Converse hi-tops just like mine doesn't

want to talk to me. He's a doctor
and he wears them all the time, he wants
me to know. Not just to sock-hops.
Between the pagers and cell phones
it's like Christmas in here. Christmas
for perverted elves. Their orgasmic
cries echoing in the gym. Well,
at least I don't have one of those.
I'm duking it out with myself.
I dance with my daughter
like a boxer in a clinch with a midget.
She's laughing. She has lots of friends here.
Not even one Elvis. The limbo contest
deteriorates. No one wants to go
that low. I'm ready to burst into laughter
or tears or maybe just burst.
The teachers are good. They know
my children, notecards full
of information on them. My son
is running in circles, trying perhaps
to wear out my strange guilt.
Two girls are chasing him.
It'll be alright, I tell myself.
I run my hands through my hair
and smell the grease. I roll
spare after spare. The Big John Santucci
memorial bowling shirt hangs loose
around me like parachute. I'm landing.
I will land. I continue to land.

THE SOUND OF IT

When my mother gave my father a back rub
in their bedroom, we had to turn up the TV
and behave. *We* offered to give him
back rubs. He claimed it wasn't the same.

I got engaged when I was nineteen. $300 ring
from the mall jeweler. When she went on vacation
with her family, I kept a pair of her panties
under the front seat of my car.

After we broke up, I could still talk her into a back rub
now and then, shamelessly invoking history
like some pompous prime minister. She disappeared
with an old friend of mine—not old enough, yeah. . . .

My back gets a little sore just thinking about it.
My mother has steel rods in her back now.
She can't bend at the waist. They sleep
in separate rooms so they don't keep

each other up. I sold the ring for $50. The jeweler
said he was giving me a deal. That I'd paid for the setting,
not the gold. They'd melt it down, reuse the diamond.

My mother stored condoms in her jewelry box.
Once I unrolled them and called them "finger gloves."
I filled them with water at the sink. She didn't
say a word. She was cooking dinner.

It all melts down again, even the steel in my mother's
back. We are all still alive somewhere, metal detectors
going off as we step through our lives. I wish
they could still escape into that tiny room,

one bed squeaking. When I'm having back trouble,
the doctor tells me *Backs are funny,* as if that explained
everything. *Rank your pain on a scale of one to ten.*

That girl is in her forties now, like me.
She had beautiful breasts, though I'm not sure
I ever told her so. They're called massages now—

perhaps that sounds more soothing. From behind,
I saw my parents hold hands last year, my mother
leaning against her cane with her other hand.
They were walking down a path toward a waterfall.

The sound of it drowned out everything.

SHOW AND TELL

My son shone our AAA magnetic flashlight
on our old globe loaded with obsolete countries
as I gently spun it, crouched in front
of his classroom. Morning here, night
there, summer here, winter there. The sun wobbled
in his grip. We pretended to call around the world
and ask the time of day and what people were
doing. I noticed my own hands trembling
as I pressed the numbers. We gave out chocolate globes
as treats. My son handled the questions
confidently. He talked about what the moon
would be thinking. Nobody asked about
the lost hours.

The University of Wisconsin Press Poetry Series

Ronald Wallace, General Editor

The Low End of Higher Things
David Clewell

Show and Tell: New and Selected Poems
Jim Daniels